The Cyclist
and His Shadow

The Cyclist and His Shadow

A Memoir

Olivier Haralambon

Translated by François Thomazeau

A Univocal Book

Published in association with
The Cycling Podcast

University of Minnesota Press
Minneapolis

So very grateful to Bernard Chambaz—I know I owe him everything. And brotherly thanks to Philippe Bordas for hosting my efforts. —*O. H.*

Originally published in French as *Le coureur et son ombre* by Olivier Haralambon; copyright Premier Parallèle 2017

Published by arrangement with 2 Seas Literary Agency

Translation copyright 2022 by François Thomazeau

Published by the University of Minnesota Press
111 Third Avenue South, Suite 290
Minneapolis, MN 55401-2520
http://www.upress.umn.edu

ISBN 978-1-5179-1373-1 (pb)

A Cataloging-in-Publication record for this book is available from the Library of Congress.

Printed in the United States of America on acid-free paper

The University of Minnesota is an equal-opportunity educator and employer.

28 27 26 25 24 23 22   10 9 8 7 6 5 4 3 2 1

Sweat came over me: do you want to see racing stars glow red? And, standing, hear the humming influence of milky stars and swarms of asteroids?

Arthur Rimbaud, *The Righteous Man*

Contents

Foreword
Richard Moore

This is a book that only a Frenchman could have written.

I mean this in the nicest way, even as a compliment. The language, although it has been beautifully translated by François Thomazeau, is French. The sensibility is French. The themes and preoccupations are French.

How did The Cycling Podcast become involved in publishing it?

On the last day of the 2020 Tour de France, François, Lionel Birnie, and I were having lunch outside a brasserie in Paris. This has become a bit of a ritual, one that is both happy and sad. It always provides a moment for celebration and reflection over our *salades de chèvre chaud,* but in 2020 all emotions were heightened. The Tour had been delayed by two months because of Covid-19, and it took place in a strange, sometimes sterile atmosphere. We felt lucky to be there at all but melancholic, too. The final stage in Paris is always like this: the race is over and at the same time not quite over, and the prevailing sense is of anticipated nostalgia not dissimilar to the last day of a vacation.*

Throw in an ongoing pandemic, and in 2020 we felt this even more keenly, as well as feeling uncertain about the future. Which might be why our discussion over lunch was dominated by precisely that topic—the future.

Not explicitly, of course. But perhaps to try and will ourselves into feeling more confident about whatever might be coming, to set down some markers or points to focus on and aim at, we discussed ideas and plans. Books came up. We had made an episode during the Tour about *The Rider,* Tim Krabbé's semi-autobiographical book written from the perspective of a rider in a road race in the Massif Central. It is a brilliantly vivid read, hailed by many as the best book ever written about cycling.

François disagreed. True, he had never actually read *The Rider,* but—bof!—this was a minor and rather irrelevant detail. In his opinion, nothing could top *Le coureur et son ombre (The Cyclist and His Shadow)* by Olivier Haralambon.

Lionel and I were intrigued. We had never heard of the book or the author, but we did know two things about François: he doesn't offer praise lightly and he is a man of impeccable taste. For this we could vouch, having spent

---

* *Reporting on the Tour de France is nothing like being on vacation, honest.*

several Julys traveling around France eating in restaurants and drinking wine that he had carefully selected.

Reading François's translation of *The Cyclist and His Shadow* evoked similar sensations. It was like tasting a rich *jus.* It was exquisitely constructed, as complex as a fine red wine, and it left a long, lingering, and very satisfying impression. It was certainly a text to be savored, to take your time over, not to be rushed. As soon as I finished the manuscript I wanted to go back to the beginning and start again (this is where the food and wine metaphor breaks down—or does it?).

The writing is dazzling. It is audacious and at the same time intimate, starting with an invitation to you, the reader, to "ride along with me because I want to open up my skull."

And boy, does he. Haralambon recalls as a teenager sleeping and even showering(!) with his bike, as well as spending "hours lying on the carpet stroking the braking surface or the butter-smooth anodizing of my gray 'service course' rims." Reading this, I felt pangs of nostalgia for my old Mavic GP4s: "butter-smooth anodizing" is perfect.

I am sure I will not be the only one to read passages of this book and blush slightly in recognition of descriptions that ring true.* The way that the imagined act of riding a bike seeps into normal life, for example: "He cannot walk

---

* *I have never taken my bike into the shower.*

up stairs, step by step or two by two, without the obsessive thought of a change of gear or cadence."

This is a book about obsession, the nobility of suffering and striving for perfection. Trigger warning: there are provocative passages on doping ("I find their incredible disdain for their own health moving") and the vogue for data ("as though the measurement of performance is seen as more real than the performance itself"). Some will nod along while reading of the diminishing powers of the aging cyclist: "When I stand up on the pedals to tackle a climb, the sway of my front wheel is not as sharp and neat as it used to be."

Reading this book, I can see and understand cycling and cyclists, including myself, in new ways. I know I will keep returning to *The Cyclist and His Shadow*, searching for a description, a line, even a word that captures the essence of the thing better than any other I have read—or succeeds by simply describing it in the most poetic way.

François was right. Of course he was.

Translator's Introduction
François Thomazeau

The question returned several times while The Cycling Podcast team was touring Britain to spread the word in theaters near you: what is the best cycling book you ever read?

I often mentioned Paul Kimmage's *A Rough Ride* not because I am a great fan of Kimmage in person but because it was the first honest, authoritative, and credible take on the extent of doping that plagued the pro peloton and it was a revelation for most. It also was available in English.

Whatever its qualities, *A Rough Ride* was overshadowed in my personal hall of fame by the publication in France in 2017 of *Le coureur et son ombre,* the small and dense book you now hold in your hands. I had never heard of Olivier Haralambon, even though he was familiar to lots of my friends riding in bunches in Bois de Boulogne, Paris, every Sunday. A publisher friend called me to say she was about to publish a great book about cycling. It sounded pretty odd to me as she had never been a great fan of cycling—or of any sports, as far as I could tell. It was not without some reluctance that I started to read Olivier's manuscript. And it was a revelation. Once I started it, I really could not put it down.

I remembered writing a TV film script titled *Contre la montre* (Against the mountain) shortly after the Festina scandal in 1999, and the director kept asking me: "What does a rider feel when he's on his bike, what does he think about in the peloton, how much does he suffer?" To be honest I never really held the answers to those questions, having never been close to being a professional rider myself. *The Cyclist and His Shadow* solved the riddle. Reading Olivier's book takes you into the very flesh of bike riding, it leads you straight into the noises, the sights, the smells, the urges involved in leaving the upward position for the stoop in the saddle. But it also takes you into the saddle itself, into the frame and the cogs and even the road, the tarmac, the rain, and the sweat. It is more a book to feel than a book to read. As Richard Moore said after going through the first draft of my translation: "It is very sexual." It is indeed. And I must admit I have seldom read such a precise and detailed introspection, not into the mind and heart of Olivier as a person but into what turned him into a member of a very special species: a rider. It is deeply personal, sometimes obscure, oddly philosophical, and certainly very French. It is a gem of a little book for the keen cyclist, of course, but also for anyone with even the slightest interest in the sport: for, as Olivier puts it, cycling is much more than sport. Much more than a way of life. It is a different way of being. And it is that very difference that Olivier is introducing you to.

Now, go ahead, take his slipstream, let yourself be driven from start to finish in this exciting ride of a book. It will probably make you smile, shiver, and wonder, but it is guaranteed to make you feel like you are outside, riding along with him. While Kimmage's was a rough ride, Olivier's is definitely a pleasant one, puzzling and disturbing at times but always fascinating.

I am really honored I was given the chance to translate this book into English and take it to an English-speaking audience. I hope you will find as much pleasure discovering it as I did. And if you ever have the opportunity to meet Olivier Haralambon in person, in a bookshop or on the road, beware. He is a hell of a nice person to talk to and a much better rider still than he pretends to be!

The Cyclist
and His Shadow

1
My Pet Shadow

Sunday morning is when it happens, more than any other day. At the time of the first church service, you come across those small moving congregations obviously in a hurry to leave the gates of the city behind them. Cyclists riding in bunches before the day has completely risen, whatever the weather. Most of the time, they are misunderstood, those men and few women whose strange colorful outfits are so tight that they betray every single fold in the skin—so tight indeed that they seem precisely designed to lay claim to the flaws of the body. They are intriguing, those figures perched on the uncertainty of their thin wheels. Their body or their shadow, which one comes first and defines the other? They are quite amusing, with their funny hats and huge sunglasses.

As a matter of fact, for whoever is not fond of it, cycling remains an oddity. Most of the time, the word brings back a few famous names, sometimes coupled with outdated first names, who have no more substance than apostles in a painting. Of course, Jacques Anquetil, Louison Bobet, or Raymond Poulidor probably had faces, but they are no longer familiar, no more than schoolchildren today could recognize Balzac or Flaubert in a picture. And most are unaware that Eddy Merckx was even better looking than Elvis Presley.

Only the overwhelming Tour de France retains a place, however irrelevant, in the complicated framework of our memories. When French is your native language, it is indeed impossible to avoid being impregnated by the Tour, but frequently what we know about it is little more than bored small talk. Cycling and the Tour belong to the background of July, a little like the color of the sky and the sand or the long-awaited warmth of the wind brushing your throat or silently creasing the surface of thick grass. The noisy background of the television, when you stretch in front of the screen in the hotter hours in the light filtered by blinds. Who never fell asleep in front of a Tour de France stage?

In the eyes of many, cycling races are a dreadfully monotonous spectacle. Watching the repetition of the same identical movement for hours, tens of thousands of times—what is the point? You might notice that the pace of their legs varies, that they accelerate sharply from time to time, that they stand up on the pedals and then sit back in the saddle; you might, should you know the toughness of some climbs at a given place, roll your eyes at the speed at which they tackle them, but you quickly get tired of it. After a puzzled pout of disbelief, halfway between respect and pity for the sight of their suffering faces, you look away and turn to something else.

Pedaling appears to be the most mechanical activity there is. A movement everyone possesses as soon as, in childhood, we learn to stand on two wheels. Is not the bicycle actually doing most of the pedaling, since it only requires following the neat, almost solid trail established by the rotation of the crank? Some even say that the effort, so simply interlocked with the cogs of the machine, is produced by dopers. So what remains to admire or amaze if even the willpower and the passion that drives them are somewhat mechanical and the difficulty a bit contrived?

Truth be told, there are many answers to those questions. There are in fact so many and they are so rich and so deep that you tend to back down instead of attempting to give them all. For in fact, as a result of an era obsessed with identical replications and objectivity, sport commentaries often gravitate around a short list of clichés confining riders to a clumsy form of black-and-white thinking (the worthy and the cheats) and identifying a few ready-made race scenarios that can be repeated endlessly. Such a systematic dimension produces a sort of gibberish meant for the people in the know or those wishing to be, but very unlikely to spur the beginner's curiosity. In the end it even becomes an obstacle. You vaguely hear about "sprints," "climbers," and "escapees," or even *chasse-patates* or "echelons," and you focus more on the jargon than on the event. As for the cycling race proper, you still don't have a clue, you still don't get it.

As for me, I was fatally bitten early on. I started pedaling and racing shortly before the age when the voice breaks and sexual desire suddenly turns the world upside down. I sometimes suffered from the slight contempt, or misunderstanding, toward an activity that was central to my life and that would soon grow to the point of invading my entire self and taking over my daily routine.

So now that I have progressed a little bit in my existence, now that I have moved some distance from the orthorexia and nearly sectarian prescriptions that for so long ruled my life, I would like to ride along this path again. I would like to become fully aware of or rather embrace the list of enchantments I had the chance to experience by being around only riders for years, by living only with them, by living only like them to the point, I believe, of becoming one myself. *Ad vitam.*

Oddly enough, the bike that made me suffer so much also showed me the most optimistic perspective in which I was ever capable of settling down. Of course, I loved pedaling breathlessly beside the demon of my shadow—it

was my pet, it was biting my legs every time the light gave
it a chance, I pulled it behind me mercilessly for tens of
thousands of kilometers and it never ever let me down.
I sweated, cried, spat, came, dribbled, bled sometimes
on the tarmac and the landscape. I have loved the bike
and I have loved racing fiercely because they gave me a
form of trust in the unfathomable immensity of life, in
the verticality of time. Without it, without them, I would
never have had the slightest feeling of eternity—not as a
myth but as an experience.

Of course, as I improved with time and a lot of
training, I was amazed by my own capacities. Never would
I have thought as a kid that my legs could one day exhale
so much heat and power. There were times when I thought
myself indefatigable, insensitive to pain—the long rides on
an empty stomach, the hills you climb a hundred times,
the scorching heat that does not even dry up your tongue.

But because it was precisely, exactly, where I did not
expect it to be, the cycling I am writing about can possibly
arouse some unexpected curiosity. Thanks to the bike,
thanks to the daily, almost desperate practice of cycling
(you never hope as strongly as when you are desperate),
the pillars of my life were revealed to me. A lot of the
things I was expecting from my elders, from my teachers,
from school or books, were fed to me freely by cycling
and cyclists: my idea of the body, of time (or eternity, as
I said), my ability to handle anguish or the destructive

effects of melancholy, but above all else my idea of the intelligence of others. Because—and it is something that is not well known and possibly the missing key—the best competitive riders are among the cleverest and the most subtle individuals in the human race, even if too often they let themselves be convinced of the opposite and are totally ignorant of their own finesse. I was forced to admit the obvious: reading nourishes you but does not make you smarter. Racing does. One of the virtues of cycling races is to prove you wrong. You think that nothing is as simple, as automatic, as pedaling or you believe that a cycling race is like *Modern Times* but without Chaplin and the poetry. You don't know a thing. Few suspect that being strong and riding fast are two completely different things, for instance. That you wrap the pedal, that you stroke it much more than you press on it. That maintaining the effort and suffering the pain mean learning to brush the pedal after opening under it, and clinging to its rim, the inner well in which it bathes and threatens to drown you.

In fact, once again, you can't see a thing. You think they are brutes while they are as delicate as ballet dancers and more astute than many writers. Otherwise they would not ride on. But their body language is not easy to read because the laws of appearance are such that you believe that their bodies are hindered by the machine and because you convince yourself that they are moving into a restrained and narrow space as a result. Children of emphasis and amplitude, you don't see a thing because they are not gesticulating. I was a kid myself, kneeling in front of the TV set when Bernard Hinault became world champion after surging on the Domancy climb. It would take me many years and lots of disappointments to understand the amount of delicacy deep inside the body and behind the fierce features and the disheveled hair of the Breton. Likewise, the thicker riders, more suited to the windy and badly paved courses of the Northern races, are as subtle in their touch as ballerinas: Paris-Roubaix and Capezio are in the same league! But nobody seems to know.

Great works have been written—I'm thinking of Paul Valéry—about dancing and the body. And of course, we shouldn't forget the wondrous cycling tales spilled from the ink pen of Antoine Blondin and many others in his wake. But too colorful a style often blurred the shades and ignored the absolute, limitless way to ride that turns training into asceticism and performance into a kind of gnosis. Too often, champions were celebrated only in the naive light of their pure achievements—or worse, of their success—without recognizing how they were motivated by their unhappiness, their *taedium vitae*. Races are now commented on only in the categories of vulgar moralism or naive scientism in denial of evidence—if those men sometimes drift apart (via doping practices especially), they often fall or sin because of "too violent a desire to be closer to God" and because "evil is only perverted good."

Ironically, what they are blamed for is what should be forgiven. They are grossly misunderstood.

Competitive cycling is too large and too lively to be restricted to an object of knowledge. I want to bow in front of such mystery. And since in the end such reflection requires a profound introspection, what I ask of my readers, besides their forgiveness, is to follow along and ride with me because I want to open up my skull to them. This box of bones is the only place where performance takes place, where it enlightens, where its world takes its various shapes.

Dancers, acrobats, sailors, writers, bullfighters, poets, artisans of effort, mystics, ascetics, whatever you like, but not athletes.

Forget about sport.

2

Flat Cosmos

He was really small and the bike very big. Already distraught. Taken away from all notions of time and place, he pushed the strange machine forward by a few centimeters—maybe he even dared a meter? Immediately the clicking crept into him, as if the ball-bearings of the freewheel were beating one by one directly onto his eardrum, somewhere deep inside behind his wide-open eyes. As if wanting to protect it, he slightly shrugged his shoulders around his shivering head. The unbelievable thinness of the surfaces resting on the ground and the intimidatingly precarious balance acquired only through speed and sharp movement totally broke his world apart.

We were all born through oblivion. Some of the cracks and tears we go through, taking with us our whole package of flesh, close up forever. We can no longer see the dead leaves still fluttering behind our back. Already we must watch our next step. I cannot believe that there is a rider who did not experience the same feeling of awe and bewilderment. Who would be unable, a few hundred thousand kilometers further down the road, at the time of the final breath, to ride back through the maze of memories down the lane leading to that first moment of amazement.

I don't know a single rider who, throughout the course of life, does not feel the temptation to fall once again for that perfection that is the bicycle as if cycling for the very first time. Even after decades of being engrossed in the naive entertainment, in the films and pictures making up most of the tragic tale of cycling, you can never relive the original scene without blinking from the incandescent light it brings back to mind. The first race bike we come across (but all bikes are *race* bikes) always seems to come down from a blinding heaven, along with glittering bouquets.

I can see as in a dream, on some of the Sundays of my childhood, constellations of dust swirling around the dim light of a room, a door, or a cellar, between the frames and the spokes. Blades of light cutting through space. And for what remains in me of my childhood calf muscles, I can still feel them harden and, without shaking, lift my heels. And I can still gauge the weight of my hand as I raise it before putting it on the salty leather of the saddle. Falling down on the cold tubes of the machine, my palm slowly runs along its spine and along the whole frame down to the last little bones. The bike that took my innocence still contracts my tongue today. On its cold and metallic body, I was tirelessly opening and closing my sweating skin, stroking the angular shape of the thin figure of steel. It was a Mercier: its white letters were sticking out on the deep pink, the pink color of meat; I can still feel its taste and its smell. I often wonder where it is now, having suffered for so long away from me, having endured different hardships. I imagine cracks and swells on its painted surface.

I also know that even the stupid plastic teat closing down the bottle attached to the frame is probably engraved in me as some archaic element of my sexuality: through the same orifice, I drank most of the water that is part of me. I pressed those plastic bidons like breasts sticky with sugar, my head back down on the side, keeping an eye on the road and my line. I'm made of shaken waters, rattled by the grain of the road. It does not help you settle down. Not a corner of still water is left inside me. Riders are made of oceanic swell.

There have been a thousand attempts to express the poetry of this object, but the bicycle resists; there were a thousand fingers pointed toward that strange little flat cosmic system. There were microscopic descriptions (but no magnification is good enough) of the subtleties of that universe we had to straddle. We know that each point in the rims gravitates around the hubs, the same as each of the fifty-three cogs around the axis of the crankset, the starting point of the whole system. And we know that at the end of its lever, the pedal draws a more distant course, on which a living foot, separated from it by the width of a sole, is going to imprint on it its own imperfect elliptic orbit. The crowns of the crankset and the teeth, linked by the chain, the pedals taking the feet along with them, move around with the wheels and wrest this whole set of orbits out of immobility. Already, the human body is called upon and, with its articulated segments, soon joins this complex and cyclic system. This urge fills the rider's stomach with a violent love.

The bike is not without some beastly aspect, as its handlebars could easily be turned into horns and its saddle into a skull or a trophy to be hung on a wall. And like a bird's skeleton, its frame is pneumatic. It abhors fullness and is hollow by essence. It holds together thanks to rigid tubes and supple tubes rolled around the wheels, which guarantee smoothness and silence. The loose air captured in its tires ensures a firm contact with the ground and a sweet contact with the world. Created by thought, the bicycle is a slight animal. Its simplicity is its strength, because there is no room for complexity. And while it remains pared down, it has already attained perfection: it is final and impossible to improve.

These days, craftsmen are gone and so are the bikes

imbued with their caresses. The legendary Marcel Borthayre died with his tricks and his twists, a man who every day, when the time came to start his work, would touch the wheels he was building only with the back of his hand for fear of "frightening them." And his father before him carved and modeled the saddles of champions after burying the leather for weeks under a tree in the garden or drowning it in wine and sage to nourish and soften it. Today, for the most part, our wondrous machines are the result of a process of industrial fabrication separating the conception and the production. The thinking of a designer on the one hand and the work of little hands on the other, carefully placing the insets of black fabric—for now most frames are made of carbon and have lost a bit of their singularity since they are set into molds. The advent of carbon fiber and composite materials was a great wind that swept over the production of the bicycle, but such changes were only skin deep.

An unbelievable amount of improvements have been added to the machine, which weighs only six to seven kilos now if it claims to be in its best shape, which resists without bowing to the merciless jumps of the sprint giants, whose derailing neatly clicks into place thanks to electronically controlled *derailleurs,* whose carbon rims are so high they cut through the wind like shields . . . the list would be too long. But it is always in glimpsing the lines of a bicycle's geometry that cyclists fall to their knees in awe. Change a small detail, lower the tip of the saddle or the spot of the brake levers by an inch, and everything collapses, the eroticism goes and the technicity of the machine takes over. When the bicycle's geometrical beauty catches the cyclist's eye, it's a good bike.

At the time of my first races, when I was a teenager, my bike would rest its tired soul in my bedroom. I would put it on a kind of tripod to clean it and I could move it around from my bed. On my back, I would turn it over with the tip of my toes and its shape would cut through the backlight in the blindness of the bare bulb blurring the material reality of the ceiling. The slow rotation would bring it closer to me on a bed of hypnotic clouds created by the blazing filament and send me gently to sleep. I would then seize it in my dreams and, in the twirling of images, I could see us winning all our races. I spent hours lying on the carpet stroking the braking surface or the butter-smooth anodizing of my gray "service course" rims, or sticking my finger in the channel dug on the cranks that were exactly the same size as my forefinger. I saw myself grow, literally; I saw the reflection of my nose get hideously bigger in the chrome-plated lugs binding the tubes and which I polished frantically with a cloth. I would press my cheeks against the cold metal. I would set up my beautiful machine and light it lovingly, a bit like I today dream of being able to photograph flawlessly the infinite landscapes of my wife's body. I would partly take it out of the darkness and move it so that thick massive shadows would pour out here and there. I would turn my mouth close to it to see my breath land on the gloss of the metallic alloys. Back from training, I would take it with me in the shower, soap it with a sponge and a brush, stretching my legs to avoid the leaks of the degreaser with which I was cleaning the chain with the help of a toothbrush. I would delete most of my traces before the return of my mother, who was coming home from a day's work only to discover a whole new list of painful tasks ahead.

Now that time, even more solidly than space, has taken me away from that bike, my hands still retain a clear memory of it. I can still run the tip of my fingers around it in every detail like on the body of a loved one, the smooth and the rough of it, the hot and the cold parts, the surfaces and the nooks.

Cycling is not a choice. It is as imperative as desire and love. Like that of a lover, the mussed-up hair of the would-be rider stood on end and his legs failed him at the first sight of a bike. From that moment, there was only one fate left to contemplate: to court, marry, absorb, incorporate that promise of speed. And turn the machine in front of him into no less than his very own flesh.

3
The Finger of St. Thomas

We equip ourselves with two wheels, because some of us are missing a half, or at least a part of ourselves. Born in the skin of those spherical creatures mentioned by Aristophanes, whom Zeus cut in two pieces as a punishment, we cured the original woe by pedaling.

The time trial of the mirror stage still remains uncomfortable for me. My reflection from head to toe displays a rather robust body still, but aging already. And the attacks of time, far from blurring its singularity, reveal more and more obviously the way it was built up.

Asymmetrical and fleshless shoulders, skin-deep hip bones, unfinished pectorals that seem to leave the skin, all these shades coming up to the surface, instead of hiding the fact unveil it: my body is a cyclist. And yet I don't ride as much anymore. And yet the tan lines are gone. Even the surface of my body hints at it, the blue and purple scars on the hips, the knees and the elbows—on everything that sticks out. The awkward and clumsy demeanor, the blushing epidermis, the sharp outlines and the slight droop, everything I see points to its absence: my standing reflection should be on a bike! And now, naked in the bathroom, I can fight my anxiety only by turning around by forty-five degrees and, by leaning my chest on a raised leg, adopting a rider's posture. My palms are missing the taped handlebars, while the absence of the chain and wheels, as it brings me back to the ordinary wobbling of the world, is painful. My missing limb is made of grease and metal, rubber and air pressure; without it I'm crippled.

It is finally quite risky, even futile, to try to understand the world or life as a series of consecutive events. There is no explaining as a consequence the intensity of the pleasure provided by riding a bike, because to go from being a pedestrian to becoming a rider is an entire modification of the being. After all, was it not necessary to stand up on our legs, to unfold completely and nod atop the high grass to deserve the name of human? To maintain with the ground that intermittent and binary link that is the essence of walking and to give it up consciously to set it up on the fragile suction of wheels: this is enough to give a child the impression of moving away from destiny.

The world you touch with two wheels is not the same as the one you touch with two feet. Relying on your wheels means perching on tiny surfaces, so tiny that they come down to simple dots when the tire is inflated hard. It means perching on two pins sliding on the road and which will soon become as sensitive and reliable as the pulp of your fingers testing the ripeness of a fruit.

I was not really a town boy, or in any case not the big swarming city that bustles so much it makes your eyes and ears bleed. I grew up quietly, in the discreet boredom of suburban limbo, in a tasteless and almost climateless environment, behind an ill-fitting window from which I breathed all the cold air that my lungs could store. The hypnotic rustle of a row of wet poplars crept around me and for a long time their smell of rotten roots was the only nature I knew. Even today, wet leaves sticking to the tarmac bring back the smell of my bedroom. The road would become blacker and shinier when it rained and was stained with petrol as spring and summer settled down. And that was about it. I was not bored to death and I was not dreaming of the countryside or breakaways. No, no. I was content with that concrete languor and with the sight of a curtain of trees so close it was nearly eating up the entire horizon. Three streets were drawing up three short perspectives converging toward a small house whose lackluster existence I was watching from my third floor.

For my project of leaving suburbia to take shape, and to exchange the formless body that awaited me there for that of a cyclist, I needed my child bikes to be replaced by a beautiful ten-speed, whose sublime spangled paint and chrome-plated rims instantly brought a cloth to my hand.

That morning I had gone in the wake of an uncle who was showing me the way. It was a winter Sunday and I was doing my best to follow him in the timid morning light; we were riding with runny noses, each in his own thoughts and the little misty plume of our breaths. I was thinking that from above, a small shape following the wheel of a larger one, I probably looked like some lost animal, moving in the open between two distant thickets of trees.

Let us be fair: I had already seen the countryside run past from my backseat view in my father's Renault, appearing like a still life painting during my bouts of holiday boredom. But I had seen it without noticing it, I had only seen it with my eyes and I had actually never touched it. I was still a small-town boy, a tiny cyclist only exploring boulevards and side streets, dead-end lanes and parking lots, letting the air brush my throat. But that day, I could feel the country fast approaching as we left behind the traffic lights of the city and the streets lined with facades. Before the immense horizon stretched freely in front of us in an ample movement, I could already sense its presence without spotting it yet, like the swelling and growling sea, in the same way you can feel the ocean while still on a side street in a seaside village. The barren line of the horizon was there already and it was shaking up the last buildings, I could almost hear it. I was pedaling in the slipstream of my uncle's solid legs falling by each side of the chain, my own feet pressing the pedals with the busy stubbornness of the beginner, when all of a sudden I found myself in the fields. Everything else had been left behind. Breathless, isolated in my own echoes by the wind, my fingers stiff and my eyes full of tears from the cold, I found myself in a blurred and muffled yet terribly real world. At one stage, the road, probably narrow, appeared narrower still and seemed to lead into an ocean of thick earth, thick to the point that the plowed furrows looked on the cusp of overflowing. The swelling glebes might have spread and drowned me with the patience of waves, aware that they would eventually force the highest cliffs to give way and topple the proudest castles.

I held my focus on the teeth of the cogwheel of the bike ahead of me, on the red struts between them. I was riding away from those misleading visions and finally settled with each kilometer into a delicious impression. I was moving ahead in the wet creases of the landscape like a mouth licking and exploring the skin wherever it hid. Exactly as in love, I was starting the construction of a new body, I was weaving a new skin for myself. Like in love in front of someone else's body, something in the landscape wrapped up around me and forced me to look inside.

I recognize now that on my bike I did not have my vision restored but I discovered what it means to see. Such a discovery can probably happen in many different ways, but as far I am concerned it was offered to me as a cyclist. You often hear that you need to lean down to look like a rider but this is doubly wrong. First because, apart from the moments when, by ducking for a few seconds, the rider gathers up mental strength, a rider is only worthy of the name by the talent to see the race, to always keep nose up even in the hardest efforts, so that none of the spasms running through the body of the peloton elude him. And more fundamentally because there is a way to see that requires not looking anywhere. The eyes of someone inspecting the quality of a fabric with the tip of the fingers are always looking into the distance because, oddly enough, to look down on the point of contact to see it more closely only makes sure nothing will appear. Reality comes alight only on the stage of our inner theater.

The morning advanced, I was pedaling, and I could feel the texture of the air thicken, stroke the skin of my neck hard, and freeze my face exactly like a layer of icing on a cake, ready to crack. In front of me, always the same back and forth pendular movement of my uncle's rustic legs around the silent rotation of chromes. And deep inside me, far, very far beneath the frosty overhang of my eyelids, the hardness of my hamstring rocking around the saddle around my buried anus, my burning legs, the alternative, periodical crushing of the soles of my shoes on the pedals, on the road, and finally on the world from which I had the impression I was finally taking something away. I was convinced I was extracting the juice of existence. The road was going up, I was standing up on the pedals. When my right leg was coming down, bending the bike and shifting my two hands to the left, when the contraction of my quadriceps wrung out the warm sweat I was already feeling along my thigh, a space was opening between my sole and the world and that was the place where we were giving something to each other. I was thirteen years old, but I was born again. I was coming out, a child of the pedal. I was too present in that upheaval to find the words, but I was living it. What I was seeing as clearly as possible did not require eyes and was not in the clumps of black branches starting to drip as midday was looming, not in the houses nestled in the middle of the fields and from which were vertically rising timid gray fumes, not in the unreeling of my wet tires or in the gleaming pedaling of my uncle, not even in the smells of ice and ember so common on winter mornings.

I was not aware yet of the existence of Caravaggio's St. Thomas, whose forefinger digs almost by a phalanx into Christ's chest and who, in order to see what he has touched, to see what he has seen, looks away from the wound in amazement. His leaning posture, his face turned toward Jesus' breast have you thinking first that he is fascinated, eager to see better. But not at all. By watching more closely, more lightheartedly (the ambivalent scar opening like a womb is indeed fascinating), you comprehend that

24

The Finger of St. Thomas

St. Thomas's look is drifting off the canvas, not toward another object concealed from the spectator but inside himself. To better see what his finger is touching, to let his finger see, he must absolutely neutralize eyesight for the sake of vision. No image, just imagination. Thomas is the magnifier of what he seeks to see.

I was discovering the same way, by *seeing* the bottom of my body more clearly than the outside world, that every test is a test of touch, that there is no way out of it. A test of touch, of weight, of resistance, of effort. Senses only replicate, disguise, clarify, shape that fundamental sensation that I have never experienced so profoundly and clearly as through the activity of cycling. Therefore I found myself at the age of thirteen on a country road, in the space opened inside me by the landscape separating my eyes from my muscles. From the tip of my wheels, I had at last touched the earth, its impossible flatness, and my soul was ripped open like a fruit whose overripe flesh was a promise of infinity.

Back in the warmth of home, as if I were waking from a deep sleep, it took me time to regain my composure. I remember sitting naked on the bedside, my elbows on my knees, still overwhelmed by the dream. Everything was immersed in the kitchen smells of Sunday, and my eyes were as heavy as two metal balls, stunned by the vision of my marbled feet, turned bluish by the cold. I needed the shower to burn me, the towel to scrape my skin, I needed to frown for a while, to rub my cheeks hard in front of the mirror to close down the well inside my body and to get away from the voices coming out of it. To get back to the silence of ordinary things. To give up that strange squat that only conceals an urge to jump forward, to empty my hands by leaving the bike aside, and to impale myself again on the vertical spit of the upright position.

Every rider learns by pedaling to locate that wound inside and to tear it open fearlessly. Pedaling brings consistency to the thick and genuine void binding the skin to the world. As years went by, the wonderful mechanism of the bike supported all the alterations in the rider's development. Every mutation, the even and the odd ones, found their organization in that set-up of circles and rectitude. When we hear that the bike is a continuation of the body, that the body has incorporated the bicycle, this is because it not only prolongs the locomotion of limbs but also because the skin seems to grow and cover it fully. The rider is the opposite of a robot; there is no getting rid of the machine that nourishes and becomes his flesh. The rider feels the bike even when you can't see it, otherwise his palms and his feet, his solid yet delicate perineum, everything would be skinned, everything would sizzle in pearls of blood. When, as it happens, the rider stays a few days, a few weeks sometimes, without operating that second skin, it summons him and he jitters as if injured, as if his limbs had been severed by a blade.

The Finger of St. Thomas

He pushes on the pedals, rotates them, makes them dance, and moves ahead in the direction designed by the road lined by spectators. Some scream and gesticulate, some look astounded and keep their hands in their pockets. Yet the landscape that is the background of the show is not the real place of his meticulous effort. He performs and creates from the resonances of his solitude and carves in himself his own share of space, where the stomach literally joins the heels, the head, the legs. He works with all muscles on the rough, indistinct, and endlessly improvable material of his most intimate life. His body is a bottomless well, the epitome of a shadow and reclusion of the kind that always contains a precise and distant echo. And in that "noisy solitude," as Spanish poet José Bergamín wrote, he gives a shape to his present and to his very existence. Hanging over that depth, he moves with all his soul. And so do the others, all of them, the whole bunch along with him. They tune their bodies to the perfect balance of power and impotence, initiative and resistance, they perform from the neat and colorful burn that they pour into their flesh and that ignites their moments of eternity. This is their art.

Not because they deserve it but to have a chance to appreciate those skills we should impose a call for absolute silence and reverence as the peloton passes. The sight of two hundred extreme solitudes riding at full lung capacity into the visible world is more an event to be listened to rather than watched.

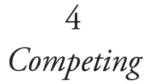

4
Competing

I can see myself from behind disappearing in an ether made thicker by my grown-up forgetfulness, my shoulders blurred and shivering along a path that I hardly understood, without any sense of direction. I had no idea that it would become the spine of my life.

How many times did my knees move up and down, pushing and pulling the pedals, since that long-forgotten day when my father or my mother, putting an end to a clumsy repetitive ride, finally let me go and left me in the hands of my own sense of balance? And how many times since that windy, drizzly morning when I took part in my first race?

It was only eight in the morning and I was waiting, with the impression I already had a long day in my legs. To become a rider, you need to compete, and I was on the brink of my first race.

Competing

My mustache still a remote possibility, I was shivering on the start line among disparate comrades, some tall, some small, some laughing out loud and some so scared they looked miserable. I was leaning forward, my forehead on my crossed arms, my elbows on the handlebars, one foot clipped into the pedal, my knee jittery and the other leg stretched. I was looking ahead from time to time, I was frowning to retain some composure beneath the lifted peak of my cap. I was looking around me. At those mouths maimed by braces, smiling all the same. At the protruding ears and locks of hair sticking out of the fragile protection of our leather helmets in the breeze. A tiny start and finish banner was flying above our heads and we were a light bunch, slightly faded by humidity, ready to ride frantically around an industrial zone in the making. The streets of brand-new tarmac were running along muddy wastelands veined with useless pipes and ducts from which stood out odd farcical ruins. The white line painted on the ground and the mucky trailer used as a podium were timid signs of life in that cold project. As I said, I was shivering. And the would-be rider was shivering inside all of us, in all those would-be bodies. He shivered even more when the punchy starter raised his gun and grinned. But he was suddenly released, from the first motion of the wheel. A silent explosion blew in my chest and then the grain of the road crept inside me through my open palms and my backside, up the nerves of my arms and the vibrating stalk of my spine, to finally spurt and blossom into my skull. From that day, like all riders, I did my best to spend as much time as possible away from the world, sheltered by that sweet rampart of familiar pain.

Before getting there, before pulling our childish and dedicated fury onto the road, we had gotten up in the darkest night. You had to have eaten the compulsory plate of pasta at least three hours before the race. Slow carbs. I had to hug the walls as I walked, groping my way toward the kitchen without switching the lights on to avoid waking up my mum. Seized the pan under the sink, put it on the stove, under the neon light. A white film on top of the water when it boiled, my eyes still dreamy, lost on the small wheat snakes drowning in the boiling water. I had opened the window to dissipate the steam. The poplars were trading jumping, singing birds. I sat alone in front of my plate, in the midst of a world still crawling out of sleep but already shaken in the distance by the engines of planes. The first Sunday in March. The first Sunday of the season.

I thought about the others, my friends in the cycling club and all the guys I did not know, all of us sitting in our kitchens in front of a bowl of pasta, like pins placed on a map. We would all soon be sitting together in a car heading out to the start line of the race. In the uterine drowsiness of daybreak shared behind a windshield, we bathed in fear and anticipation of the competition ahead.

Competing

I closed the door behind me and walked down the stairs, my bike slung over my shoulder. A few streets away, I waited in a large round square, in the first light of day, with the damp tarmac still glistening. I sat on the frame of my bike, my bag at my feet, until the old Peugeot appeared, bristling with racks and wheels like an insect weighed down by its antennae. It stopped in front of me, trembling. I fixed my bike on top of it and got in as the suspension grated, on my way to my comrades and our coach. Everything smelled of laundry detergent, camphor, and moisture.

There were fewer people at the start than there would be later. For some of us this day might be the unofficial start of elite or professional cycling careers. No buses yet, no carparks bustling with people moving up and down like spiders. No onlookers, lost in all that fuss like dead wood in a flood. No podium girls either, no pretty groupies in the bright happiness of summer. No journalists, except the guy from the local federation weekly. Not many people at all. Only the March sky and two uneven rows of family cars parked on each side of the road. The car trunks were open, the hoods lifted like huge mouths, and pairs of legs were sticking out, bare and so tender still. Behind the cars, and at the feet of their sons, fathers were kneeling, pouring oil in the palm of their left hand before kneading the flesh of their flesh like the bread it might earn someday. Their heads low, one knee down, piously bowing in front of their hairless offspring. Mothers and sisters were standing still at some distance. Here and there a plastic hairband was wrapping up some blonde hair.

As for us, it was our coach—my father was not there yet—who had given us the little massage, the revulsive cream painfully burning the skin, while we were pinning our bibs to the pockets of our jerseys. With my numb fingers, I did my best to pierce the thick paper at the right spot so that it was perfectly stretched on my back. I can't remember what my number was.

While we, the riders, were flocking on the line as our names were called, trainers and fathers had gone by small bunches, straightening their woollen caps and hats before hiding in the ditch at the spots they thought strategic. Here and there on the circuit we would see those strange waders, popping their heads to shout advice and warnings, a spare wheel in their hands.

We were all starting in the trade that very day and as soon as the gun fired and punctured our fearful hearts, we discovered the marvelous zone beyond urgency. Everything was going so fast. The fresh air brought to all our mouths, I suppose, the metallic taste of blood. Breathless before each turn, we still had to hurry up so as not to lose our place, resist the shoulder of the next guy while avoiding tangling his handlebars in ours. Hurry once more to speed up as soon as our balance permitted.

Competing

There were a couple of crashes, I saw a front wheel touch another, a rider stagger as if a stumbling drunk or a boxer before hitting the canvas in a clanking noise. First bruises, initiatory wounds—from head to toe, shoulders, elbows, hips, knees, ankles.

Bonuses were awarded each time we were crossing the line and I did well enough to stick a few coins inside my tracksuit pocket when the time came to go. Halfway through the race, I remembered my coach's warning. Stretching my arm behind my back, I grabbed the candy bar in my pocket. I struggled to unwrap it with my teeth as much as to swallow it, so short was I of breath. I spent a whole lap with a wad under my cheek, my lips shiny with sugar. As the final lap was looming, I was gathering my thoughts and cheering myself up by talking to my bike, to its beautiful blue aluminum frame. I was also thinking of Hinault and all the feverish pantheon pinned on my walls. I was praying. As I was slightly turning my head sideways when the pace was getting too high and making me suffer, I saw with the first ray of sun the reassuring sight of my shadow. It was stretching, growing, spilling over the gravel on the side of the road before clinging back to my ankles. When the final lap bell rang, we were all more determined to miss our fourteenth birthday than to give up. I probably started my sprint far too early, but I could not hold it. While I was full enough of self-inflicted fear and despair, I went on an expiration, gripping my handlebars so hard

33

that my knuckles went white. A trapped animal venturing out in the open. Standing, sitting, standing, sitting. Fear, fear, fear. For a few seconds, looking under my elbows, I saw a world upside down, with screaming fathers, their fists clenched, their heads down, moving a bent leg forward onto the road.

I was patted on the back and we, the riders, shook hands. It lasted for some time—we could not stop shaking hands. Fifteen minutes later, another hand was sticking out to put me up on the trailer, as the stepladder was gone. A young woman was standing there amid a pale blue sky, almost buried in a heavy jumper. She handed me a bunch of flowers, to me who had never offered flowers to anyone. I lifted it up over my head and my coach took a pic.

We felt like rising stars. When I arrived on my street with my flowers on my handlebars, all the neighborhood girls were at their windows, chatting and calling each other. The façade of the building looked like an Advent calendar. Behind them, you could feel the polished kitchens, the put-away dishes and the pink rubber gloves thrown over the faucets like the remains of Michelangelo in the arms of St. Bartholomew on the walls of the Sistine Chapel.

I left my bike on the doorstep and I took my shower without it. On my bed, the flowers were sweating. But I was and we all were real cyclists now.

5
Liquid Body

I don't know anything about the old man I sometimes overtake when I happen to ride again. Nothing, because he has never said a word to me. I know nothing except that he was once a good rider. When I see him, his head high, pressing on the pedal with such sharp authority, I can hardly believe his age. He still rides every day even though he does not fill his outfit entirely anymore and even the Lycra shorts fold up on his skinny thighs. On his stretching leg, the kneecap is out of proportion, and a few hems of skin sit up on top of it. Youth no longer swells or stretches the skin. White hair is sticking out of the helmet on his Faustian neck, while a slight prognathism (his teeth moving back inside his mouth), his blushing eye corners, and whitish cornea give him away. Yet those eyes reveal who he is by the way he looks up from below when he speeds up, and his shin is still oblong when he pulls, his hands half open on the handlebars and the impeccable undulation of the bike. He keeps up the pace with the tough young guys who ride along with him, and behind his ghostly disguise the rider inside him is so present that it seems destined to survive the obvious disappearance of the body.

It is not impossible that the same man started in life like one of those shy kids whose reflection in shop windows comes as a disappointment when in the company of others. Kids with sad guts. With a frame that always tends to shrivel as though a few bricks were missing in the very middle to support it. Just imagine. The posture was not good enough and our rider joined the long list of children told to "stand up straight" and "behave yourself." Incapable of standing straight or sticking out his chest for more than a second, in that regard the bicycle, a natural solution to that incurable ailment, saved him and boosted his morale. He was simply meant to click into that bent-over position. Even inside him, it was the way he felt. The comforting supports provided for his hands and ass, the paradoxical stability of the pedals that simultaneously resist and give in, the indirect contact with the hardness of the ground turned the world into a softer place. Wheels, pedals—they turn but never let you down. Their eternal return, which protects the body from shocks and replaces them by the silent rolling of the tire on the surface of the earth, creates a sweet and ambiguous place. It supports elusively and gives way reassuringly. The bicycle is essentially and geometrically inclined to paradox and oxymorons. Antoine Blondin described it—I quote him from memory—as "the most efficient instrument to help man improve the efficiency of his movements since the pole used to knock down walnuts." It is even more than that. There are certainly very few objects so suited for people with awkward dispositions, so apt to turn clumsiness into efficiency, despair into a project. The bike molds, builds, and gives a meaning to useless bodies. It is quite common that the mere act of riding a bicycle instantly enhances a nondescript pedestrian, that dejected bodies come alight and line up like living cathedrals, that lackluster people, unnoticed in their everyday guise, suddenly radiate all around. The rider's position strips them, unveils who they are. Never mind if a champion is not in competition gear: a rider is always naked.

But the life of the body takes nothing for granted. We know that the bindings of the flesh will come undone one after the other.

As I am trying to write these lines and while the window behind my back protects me against winter and the freezing hiss I would have so eagerly embraced on my bike in the past, it goes without saying that my athlete's body has gone.

Liquid Body

When I ride now, twenty years after my last competition, and even if I had trained regularly in the meantime, I am not as solid and secure a figure as I was then. My knees sometimes become shaky on the gears like a badly tuned mechanism letting pressure out and when I stand up on the pedals to tackle a climb, the sway of my front wheel is not as sharp and neat as it used to be. It is also very likely that I have become totally unable to sprint or that I would be utterly ridiculous if I did. From within, as years go by, a centrifugal force is rising that will shake me up completely if it reaches the surface. If I let it do that. Because my flesh now seems to hesitate, I am not as strong as I used to be and my determination, so acute in the past—each part of the body at just the right place—is threatening to drift away from me like the carriage of a typewriter. What is even worse is that I now progress in a thicket of procrastination growing like brambles on the ground while I am looking away, probably unwisely. That is what happens when you let your guard down, when you picture yourself at the bow of a ship, sticking your chest out in the setting sun: you cannot see where you are going. My blood is now corrupt with phlegm. I have become lazy, I keep nit-picking. The wind creeping into my collar is now a problem. Before every ride, I check closely every opening in my outfit as if my clothing were sheltering my courage. And the heat in the summer days stuns me.

As soon as I decide to ride these days, I first have the

impression that I have lost it completely. I'm moving inside a gap. The first kilometers make me feel like I am out of focus and I cannot adjust myself to my body totally; I cannot fit in. The ferrous taste of the hapless dreams I had sometimes on the nights before a race, when I could see myself riding at the back of the bunch in the creepy despair of my unheard cries, unable to progress, is coming back to me. With every training session, I need some time, even though it diminishes with each ride, to coincide once again with my own flesh. But I always manage in the end, even if imperfectly, even if a few uncomfortable wrinkles remain. I more or less settle back in. It is the whole set-up of moving supports that gradually helps me back inside myself. I dig in, I thrust myself in, I tune myself to my skin and it is the bike that I finally swallow, that I incorporate. My pedaling self is resurrected by that indirect confrontation with the world that is cycling. One stroke of the pedal after the other, I come alive. One stroke of the pedal after the other, my cycling self sustains itself through effort and strengthens its organic ties.

I am settling in, as I said. We will see, I tell myself, and if I have to struggle, I am determined to struggle with style. Something will come out of it. I pedal hence I feel. Don't panic, go ahead, your mouth between your rotating knees.

I engaged the toe clips one after the other with the neat little clicking noises I love so much. My feet found their rightful place and as usual I felt the shifting spot on the axis of the pedal right under the big metatarsophalangeal joint: "just on that spot that would allow you to crack a walnut open on the ground," one of my former coaches used to say. My hands are placed anywhere on the handlebar and the palms curl around it. They would only be spindly, those hands, and would not register anything without the bulges of flesh beneath the thumb and the little finger modulating the pressure with a slight pulsation of the grip, so slight I don't notice it anymore. The condition of the road varies all the time, as well as the proportion of my own weight ebbing and flowing at the end of my arms.

So when I ride, and while the wind dries up my itching skin on my cheekbones, while my mouth is opening in an expression I cannot visualize, my weight is divided between three pressure points—or more exactly five, because I have two hands and two feet. Depending on my attitude, on the intensity of my effort, but also on the bumps of the terrain, and especially the changes in elevation, my weight moves around my body, increasing the pressure here and reducing it there. At times the pressure intensifies in my arms (in descents, for instance) and even more so if I brake hard to take a turn; at other times most of my weight moves down to my pelvis, if the road goes up and I need to climb. And my body must constantly correct the balance.

Liquid Body

Riders move within a space both closed and modifiable, because it is limited by pressure points that are pretty loose, within a space that is fundamentally plastic and the shape of which is defined by the very effort. Their weight moves inside the airtight bag of the body frame and, like a heavy liquor or like mercury, it goes up and down. The unheralded art of the rider is to play with that backwash so as not to be stuck on the spot with each change of terrain or tactics. For that is where the main difficulty lies. Because it is not limited to biological limbs and because it definitely includes the machine, the rider's body is liquid: it must be as flexible as the water that spreads whatever happens, the water that submerges everything and that flows into every crack to get where it needs to go. It must obey and nod to what the terrain suggests in order to better divide its weight between the two wheels.

The trappings of visibility, which would have you mistake the living body for a thing if you did not look more closely, lead you to believe that pedaling is nothing and does not require any competence, that those bloody cyclists are nothing but rough strength since they move forward interlocked with a machine and that the machine is doing the pedaling since it is the one to impose the movement. Of course nothing could be more inaccurate.

Out of habit, riders see themselves as tough and brutal. They roll their dark eyes and expose formidable legs, but let's face it: the roughest of them all are only fake rough boys, feigned tough guys. Because to slide around the many bumps of the course, to make sure the ad lib repetition, for hours, of descents, sharp turns, and stiff climbs becomes more than a discontinued succession of awkward movements, you must be capable of countless and permanent adjustments, so subtle they are beyond words.

It is not often said, but to ride fast on cobbles like in Paris-Roubaix requires the delicacy of a ballet dancer. The capacity I am talking about is a knowledge of the utmost quality, combining a specific culture and a sensitivity of exceptional finesse. I kept for a long time, hanging on the wall of my bathrooms (I kept it after moving twice), a picture of Belgium's Johan Museeuw, who reveals precisely what I am talking about in 2002 in L'Arbre, one of the last cobbled sectors of the race. Usually, Museeuw does not have much in common with a ballerina (even though I saw him walk barefooted on a parquet floor and carpet after holding the door for me, and in a way his big muscular bottom was giving his step and posture as much grace as rough power) but in this case, after two hundred and fifty kilometers of rain and mud, his jersey soaked, his whole body swollen with blood by the cold, he resembles a coal miner, a hooligan, or a soldier, but certainly not a ballet dancer. Not at first sight, in any case. His features are buried in a thick crust of gray mud, his eyes look like two holes filled with egg white and his mouth like a well of flesh, outrageously pink, wet and obscene, from which probably come out, between gasps, moans he is the only one to hear, engrossed as he is in a storm of tremors, of screams and breaths spat at his face by the crowd. What we do hear as he rides past is the hiss of his bike, the rims creaking on the cobbles, and the chain slamming the shaky frame. The cable of his look, totally turned inward, is already tied to the finish line, ten kilometers farther up the road. Here, only his body speaks, utters the words of his effort on the rugged road. His pelvis is sitting way back in the saddle and it looks as though he is pushing the pedals away from him, like a man trying to kick his way out of a pile of litter.

Yet one detail attracts the eye. His hands are leaning, hardly gripping the hoods of the brakes, and oddly his little finger is sticking out, pointing outward, outside the handlebar, as if taken away, as if indifferent to the whole movement. In other circumstances, in some other picture, the same detail would mean something completely different—the same twitching finger would not be out of place on a swooning character. But it is the whole appearance of the body, because paradoxically a perfect relaxation coincides with all the tension in a furious internal dialogue and there is not the slightest hint of convulsion. In fact, the whole posture of the rider derives from the most intimate movement, even from the tiniest nervous signal given to the palms of the hands. The same happens with musicians whose bodies rear back as the strings get tighter.

When the effort reaches its peak, when the legs and shoulders get stiff, the rider can feel his hands groping for the right position, for the right grip, and the slightest modification in the handling, in the direction, the slightest movement of the fingers can change everything. If, for instance in a long climb, the rider stands up on the pedals, hands down on the brake hoods, staying for a long time without sitting back, braced upon the pedals and against the hill, the simple fact of lifting the little finger away from the other four to curl it behind the bars will bring considerable modifications to the interaction of muscular chains: rotator cuff, rhomboid major, and *latissimus dorsi* will lock up and alter the inclination of the pelvis and the whole mechanism of the legs.

But while the outside viewer can break down the movement in technical terms, the rider has to deal with the whole of the effort as a block. That is how the rider's body is felt: the pulp of the fingers and the relaxation of the soles wrapping up the course of the pedal, the efficiency of the pelvic thrust or the quadriceps, everything is made in the same mold. There is no distance, not a long way to go between what appears from the outside as the most remote parts of the whole. The body in action is a body without organs and the transformations it endures bring it back to the condition of an amoeba. It adapts as a whole and the slightest feeling of division inside it shatters the whole. And that is when the cobbles suddenly emerge from the earth like in a nightmare, like monstrous teeth sown in the ground and coming up like an army of soldiers to stop the speed and the momentum.

6
Vocation

Like all forms of science, the science of cycling comes to some more easily than to others. In this case, too, understanding it is less a matter of talent than a matter of heritage. All pelotons, from the lowliest amateurs to the professionals, include cycling siblings, brotherhoods and sisterhoods. You have the brothers and sisters of riders. Sons and daughters. Nieces and nephews. Grandsons and granddaughters. And all pass on the tricks of the trade to each other as well as the somewhat nomadic way of life that sees the family roam across the country from one race to the next. To be born into a cycling family is to learn the laws of cycling racing like you learn to speak or be clean. Taking your first steps on the roadside of a criterium, sitting between the pump and the spare wheels at the back of the station wagon in which Dad just put on his shorts and filled his bottles, and in which, after the finish, he rubbed his armpits with a tissue soaked with cologne while telling you about his race with such passion that he did not even notice that you were walking for the first time, being immersed in language by the systematic tale of such feats, is a priceless privilege. For growing beside a man with jutting ribs, who rolls the skin of his legs between two fingers to show you the way, is a predestination. Let's say that, at least, looking up in fascination, stretching your arms and saying "Dad" to a pair of trunks wrapped up with veins, or catching a glimpse in the shower of that odd two-tone nudity, is not without an influence on the future aspect of your own reflection.

In the families I am thinking of, you ride and you race as much as you grow, you join your first club as naturally as you would celebrate your First Communion in the French village churches of the past. You find yourself to be a sprinter, a climber, or a *rouleur* the same way as you would become a clown, a tamer, or an acrobat in the circus dynasties. You cannot get away from the camphor and ambulant life of the peloton any more than you can avoid the stuffiness of the big tops. Not only do you learn early the little ascetic rules—for instance, to eat only what the intensity of your training allows—or how to choose a saddle or a tire but also all the devious tricks of the race. When the dinner-table chats have always dealt with the mythological tale of the father's feats and his tactical flair, you get to the start of your first race as cunning and knowledgeable as an old dog.

On the other hand, declaring yourself one morning as the first rider of your lineage immerses you in a brand-new world. You have a lot to learn, a lot of mistakes to make. I did not spend the Sundays of my early childhood pedaling on the sidelines of a race, riding around the cars in the riders' parking lot. I did not spend my Wednesday and Saturday afternoons behind the counter of the family bike shop under a ceiling of hanging wheels and tires. I was not introduced to the secrets of crossing spokes, of the virtues of coffee and aspirin or the art of sprinting or picking the right diet. When I began as a racer, I had started riding a bike only recently and I was still busy trying on that new body bending over two wheels; I was still amazed at how wonderful it was. Yellow bubbles of soft light were still dancing in my eyes. I was leaving behind no less than another life, and being proud of it was a full-time job. I was getting carried away: it felt like I had made vows that made me different, like I had chosen a rugged, windy, hard road to travel.

The whole comedy of perspective and destiny was overwhelming. To have drifted away from an ordinary schoolboy life made me strut about. I was now claiming an everyday routine dedicated to hardship and suffering. I would be the first monk with shaven legs in my family. Physical pain was the flag I was bearing, I was not afraid of being mortified, and it was my very body, my very brutal life, that I was hoping to squeeze and wring to make a living. Hard work and headwind. I wanted my place in the family history and to struggle as hard as my father, whose unkempt hair would soon haunt the grassy roadsides of my races.

I started with the pretense that it would be my job, no less, but I did not have a clue. I was only marveling at the capacities of my body and at the longer distances I was gradually covering. From the early days of spring to the reddish glow of autumn, all my Sundays (and soon enough all other holidays) were now dedicated to competition. I was still going to school and I was training after class, more and more and better and better as the days were getting longer. On race days, I would leave the family home at dawn, my plate of spaghetti swallowed and my legs already rubbed beneath my tracksuit.

As soon as the start was given, I would feel so much pleasure from sheer effort that I was content with riding in front of the peloton as fast as I could. I was burning my forces with a kind of dedicated ardor, as if I were doing my best not to be rewarded for my hard work. Because I knew, of course, that it was a mistake and totally counterproductive tactically. I knew someone was bound to criticize me for this and I could see my father and my coach roll their angry eyes and tear their hair out. There was no need in that case to come from a cycling family to know that while I was wearing myself out with my mouth open in the gusts, the rider immediately behind me, sheltered by my back, was saving a good third of his energy. And even that the riders in the seventh or eighth positions were spending roughly half of the strength I was wasting. I was ruining my chances knowingly, aware that I would eventually call it a day and that I would hopelessly see the guys at the back overtake me without a look, the way they would ride around an old tire. Yet I was looking beneath my folded elbow and, spotting the queue of my followers, I could not think of anything better to do than operate my lever with my finger to move the chain down a gear and accelerate again. For me, it was all a matter of wind and barren horizon. I wanted to be alone on the brink of the world—nothing else mattered.

It would take me years to give up on that fable and to learn to play it a little bit better. Maybe to simply recognize that the poetry of cycling is not as naive as to hint only at martyrdom and sacrifice. And it is a good thing if the strongest rider almost never wins, because it is in the difference, in the gap between the strongest and the best that the sport becomes what it is. As it turns out, the lesson is not always within the grasp of the beginner and some of us, me included, need many a disappointment to admit it and learn to enjoy being clever. To work to beat a stronger guy.

Vocation

As he progresses with the years, a robust rider, a tough guy in solid and stupid form might be capable of explicitly dominating his peers without having to do anything more than crush the pedals at a chosen time. But outdoing the rest of the field, breaking away, taking the money and running away with each race often means facing a relatively weak opposition.

As he climbs up the ranks along with his victories, the young cocky rider will learn to curb his gratuitous efforts. Once he becomes immersed in more seasoned and faster pelotons, the gaps in which he could move freely like a beast basking in treacle become tighter and tighter. His accelerations, once fatal, become useless and ridiculous and he will survive only through learning. And through cunning. Outside the beginner ranks, you never drop anyone by riding in front of the peloton. You need to find a way to surprise your opponents to create a swift, clean break provoking that moment of confusion you can take advantage of. Force the others to reveal their flaws and strike in their moments of weakness. But to "blow them off your wheel" (to drop them when they are sheltered in your slipstream), no way—nothing more than an infantile fantasy, the anal stage of the rider. Whoever speeds up frantically with all the others in his wake is only stretching the catapult that will soon launch ahead of him, far, far away, the group of escapees in which he will not belong. The bunch at his back has been planning in his breath.

Then comes the bursting point and an imperceptible reduction in the speed. And that is when the catapult suddenly slackens. And all of a sudden, all is lost. While he looks at his feet and seeks some air, the others are gone and he will not see them again.

He can no longer crush the opposition and he has at last understood that being brave does not mean wasting his energy to no avail. And now, to give his merit a braver face than that of a tired man, the pedaling rookie will be looking for diversions: he will look outside himself for the strength now eluding him. Perhaps he will look for representations and think back on his physics classes. Or his judo lessons. To use the strengths of his rivals for his own benefit. The body you could not overthrow by standing still, and whose changes of balance and surges you must take advantage of, is the whole peloton, in one piece. The rider must learn to move with the flow and to position himself right on the lever of the catapult—inside the bucket.

But there is more to it. Once propelled to the front of the race, and now riding with the chosen few, he will have to be even more cautious. He must not show his riches, not let his treasure glitter. If a glimpse appears of what lies inside the box, he is done, he will have to pay his share. That is why he must be very careful to gently stroke the pedals, to only spend the price for keeping the pace. He must simulate pain and improvise expressions, stick his tongue out at the corner of his mouth, move his head about, even let out a bit of mucus as a sign of disarray, but without overdoing it. Basically he will play the comedy of suffering, as seriously as possible, to fool his opponents and to avoid pulling too hard. While the race can spread over four, five, or six hours, the game is to save the best for last. To savor and preciously preserve the spark. To tend to the flowing flames of the fire. You don't attack twice: it has to be neat and cut into the body of the bunch to claim its success.

7
The Monster

The flesh must be shared. Everybody is required to give their bit. From the helicopter, you see the flow of the peloton squeeze like thick blood when the road narrows or changes direction. It splits in two like a snake slithering around the roundabouts, then gathering again and stretching on the long flat ahead.

Obviously, the peloton cannot be boiled down to its name. Because not only does it not curl around itself, as the French word suggests—and it even less evokes a small ball of yarn—but above all it is remarkably plastic, even worryingly unstable. It is malleable, and that is an understatement: it is shaped by the wind, the road, and the goals of the individuals who compose it.

At first sight, one could say it is the beautiful vision of a colorful and supple object, whose many shapes vary with the point of view. At average height or from a chosen viewpoint, standing still or moving along with it, the impressions it gives can be very different, but almost inevitably the organic or animal metaphor comes to mind.

But let's step back and take another look. It stretches and curls up, extends and contracts, it moves along the bumps and the bends, but as long as they do not spill all over the place like marbles from a torn bag, two hundred fidgety brushes paint the scales of a fabulous monster, like the dragon of a Chinese New Year.

That extraordinary skin can stretch endlessly, to the extent that even when it cracks you cannot believe that the tear is serious because the invisible ties it is made of are most solid—the terrain, the course, whose design it hugs, the hairpins that, in the mountains, give it its flowing and serpentine aspect. When the road goes up, the beast lazes on it at the slow pace of a grass snake, it files its hide on the scorching tarmac that just as quickly dries up as soon as the rain begins to pour down. That is when you see that underneath the shine of the jerseys are bare limbs and muscles shimmering with a copper glow. Along the descents, the peloton crawls down like the asp that appeared between fruit and killed Cleopatra, as the legend goes.

On the flat, the peloton regains its horizontality and rectitude, silently moving under the greatest expanse of the heavens or beneath a blanket of incoming storm. Wind is what models it now (never forget the passive dimension of the wind, for the speed of the peloton creates its own breeze). It sharpens, it stretches. It progresses, oblong and slender, trailing in its wake small wreaths of worn-out riders, it shrinks by the tail and lets go of some of its scales, abruptly pulled from its carapace.

Is the wind's confrontation with the peloton only a frontal attack? That is the only instance when the peloton deserves its branding: it becomes compact, it huddles, it moves slowly and steadily, fighting tooth and nail against the blowing enemy, like a Roman phalanx fending off another. During such moments, do not expect anything exciting sportswise: cycling becomes the literal experience of *endurance*—or even boredom, because no one is spared the ennui of those long hours shared by both the actors and the spectators. And yet, if the slightest of subtle modifications takes place, then suddenly the entire pack comes back to life. It stretches, darts like an arrow whose tip coincides with the side of the road from where the wind blows. Like biological entities in the eye of a microscope, the colorful scales of the monster position themselves across the road, shifting away from one another by half and forming what they themselves call "an echelon." Spreading the entire width of the road, the echelon functions autonomously. It splits from the mother cell in a ballet-like mitosis, and if it is not followed by a second and a third echelon (and so forth), it will naturally break away, literally lifted by the laws of aerology.

The Monster

The wind disorients and strips a few riders but also shelters and guides the others.

For just as there exists in the bullring "a square meter where death awaits," there are dangerous places in the peloton, spots where its large body falters. As an individual rider, to roam in those weak spots, to linger there, means being doomed to surely end up kicked out of the pack. In those areas, insurmountable storms are roaring, tornados lash the skin of the monster and nobody ever comes out alive. The fact that they point at well-known joints in the body of the peloton and that everybody knows where they lie does not protect against panic. If, behind the first echelon spreading across the road, a second echelon takes time to deploy, riders find themselves pulling behind each other and form a kind of loose ribbon trailing by the roadside. Since speed stretches it badly and the possibility of keeping the pace depends entirely on the slipstream of the rider in front, that comet tail puts most of those who ride in it on an ejection seat.

Woe betide the odd rider who finds himself facing the wind. He will first be shaken, then inevitably blown apart by the gusts. Unable to slip his wheel between the bike ahead and the edge of the road, arms trembling, on the verge of crashing and forced to work twice as hard to retain his berth; the unfortunate rider in such a situation knows that the last moments have come. His only chance, before breathlessness takes away skills and strength, is to fake the inability to keep up and to move slightly aside: by so doing, he hopes that the rider behind will lose nerve by seeing the gap increase and will jump blindly, and in his place, into that hostile windswept pocket.

Gods willing and wind falling (or if the race goes through a crease in the landscape sheltering the bunch), the peloton swarms, gathers up, mills around, and vibrates again as it counts its losses. You can then breathe for a minute, exactly as you would rest your back in a trench waiting for the next charge (and, indeed, when you see it approaching from the front, a roaring melee shielded behind walls of dust, it is easy to mistake the peloton for a plundering horde).

It is important to understand that such a lifeform, which takes the various shapes of its environment, swallows riders and spits out others, obeys organic principles. The peloton exfoliates by the front and the back. The dropouts yield to the fatal languor reigning in its trail, while it ejects with a violent sneeze the most efficient riders to the front. As for bunch sprints, they are its climax, a last spasm ejaculating winners on the finish line. For from being shaken and rattled for so long, climbing one by one the rungs of the pleasure ladder, its wild power to choose and promote its own prophet comes.

The Monster

There you are again on the side of the road, standing clumsily in clover and couch grass. Here it comes. Half-close your eyes, softly. That's the way to do it—you must get rid of the misleading clarity of the outlines—that's the way to see the peloton as it is, to feel it march past with the gentle whirlwinds it creates. Breath and dust. You are beginning to understand. That huge, noisy, sweaty, and smelly animal is much more than the sum of the impeccable bodies it is made of—and is probably something completely different. Feel, behind the sparkle of the deep colors, the hazy patina that makes the light darker. While those glittering, shiny legs rush past under your nose, while those half-naked men flash by, whitewashed by the summer or gilded by the fall, the thrill you feel comes from one and the same flesh. Like every living creature, the bunch leaves behind it the deafening void of its absence, a space emptied by its passing, in which suddenly everything has died down.

Its cohesion is so real that the limits of the individual are porous. Skewered by the marrow, every rider sheds some blood in the melting pot of the peloton's formidable heart, puts existence and breath at the service of the monster with a hundred mouths. Even when you consider those who ride apart from one another, the effort of a rider is never totally independent from the efforts of all the others. The hydra has the dimensions of the sea and the fluidity of water. It emulates the breathing of the ocean, a succession of swelling and shrinking, but also its duplicity, for beneath the appearance of calm on the surface, powerful forces are roaring underneath. You must patiently learn the map of those currents, year after year, month after month, if you hope to navigate safely. You must guess where they are, even if you do not know what they are, in order to make it back to the front of the peloton among the top flight without grazing your hands on the oars. You must learn to surf on those streams, to pick them, if you wish to avoid being relegated to the cheap cuts or be excreted. But you can do even better, for it is possible to stir those currents, to give birth to the wave, to lay its groundwork in order to drag yourself skillfully on top of it. And then it is the vital flow of the full body that makes the efforts in your place. This is how you break away from it, by tickling it where it hurts. Under the wheels of the skillful rider, the swell rises, then the roller stands up to throw him faraway up front, on the shore and the sand of his lonely effort. And there, once the link with the pack is cut out, he needs to build another wall around himself, settle into the inner citadel evoked by Marcus Aurelius, and tackle the consequences of his self-imposed ordeal.

8

Intimacy

The mere crossing of a white line shatters the peloton. All of a sudden, it splits apart. All of a sudden, the amazing sliding movement stops and then they reappear, like bubbles popping at the surface, myriads of colorful elements spreading among a mob of pedestrians. They put themselves in the rough and maternal hands of their *soigneurs,* who cover their backs, rinse and wipe their dusty faces, comb their hair with near-tenderness, and open the soft drinks they take to their mouths. They give themselves over to the questions fired at them and reply with a few sweaty words while they are being escorted, panting, through the maze of metal fences to which nameless hands are clinging, and then to the bus, to the shower, or—a sponsored cap on their skull—to the microphones and the cameras.

The fabulous monster is no longer rushing along the

road, but the peloton does not entirely disappear. The invisible ties knotted by the wind all day do not come off and the magical presence of the bunch still creeps around the cities and the hotels at sunset. In the lobbies, a more or less silent traffic—the discreet swish of sport shoes on the carpet—continues until late into the night. Mechanics, coaches, doctors, managers, physical therapists, journalists, officials: the care and attention the riders require are enough to occupy an army.

Cyclists live among themselves for most of the year, like a pack of hounds whose life depends on the seasons.

Before or after dinner, each of them, in turn, goes through the same door and steps into a room saturated with powerful essences, in which they strip and lie down, head first, on the cloth and the table, giving up their body like a prize, an offering on the altar. The masseur sticks out his powerful hands, soaked with oil, and grabs a foot that he puts on his shoulder. The first words come with the regular rustling of the rubbed skin. The palms go down from the sole and the Achilles tendon, the fingers dig into the thick of the shin and the thigh, the buttocks and the back of the lying body, collect the words from deep within the flesh, bring them together and push them up toward the mouth. Then, at the other end of the table, from the face buried between crossed arms, pour out the tales that spill down to the ground, the pains and the woes, the frustrations and the exhaustion that were obscuring the muscles and the future. After a long while, cleared from those patchy moods and perked up, you lift yourself up and press your hands on the side of the table while sweat is dripping from the masseur's forehead. You squeeze your refreshed legs into your trousers, leave the heady scents of pine, eucalyptus, mint, or lavender, and, through the hazy light running along the corridors, you go back to your room.

The riders share everything. Or almost. The wind and the pain, the risks and the rain, the killing heat and the never-ending stages under crushing blue skies. The adamantine emptiness of the summer skies as well as the tormented shapes of the clouds. Cycling races do not lean on a moment in the day: they take the lot. Riders live and ride. In the outbursts and the lulls of the race, it is the earthy existence that is emulated. The animal and the political life. You get dressed and undressed, you drink and you eat, you hope and you despair, you talk and sometimes fight, you pay a visit when you have not seen someone for a long time. Champions are surrounded by regards and sometimes bodyguards, bouncers you must get past to approach them. In the evening, when they no longer have a bike between their legs, their life sort of expands to a second and third circle of people—the ones they work with and the ones they are exposed to, more or less willingly. Between them, silence is the link, because the tumult of the race, whose burden they have shared, has given way to peace. They take the same buses and the same cars, run into each other in train stations and airports, carrying and pulling the same bags. They take their meals as teams and eat like well-behaved schoolboys, all dressed the same, around a tablecloth littered with fruit and boxes of cereals. Two hundred days a year, they share rooms and scents brought back in their suitcases from all parts of the world. They hang their laundry and their bandages as if they were camping in the desert, lie in their beds with their legs raised against the wall, put cream on their burnt noses and spend a long time calling home, when they have one. The TV set hanging from the wall is talking to itself. Two of them, sometimes more, try every night to destroy the block of unspoken anguish and excitement that is the silent result of their hyperactive existence. You will often find them flocking in the quilted leatherette chairs of the hotel bar, from which they sometimes bring bottles up to their rooms to enhance their reputation when it gets late, or sharing around some soporific liquid as if it were sacramental bread. Looking for ways to forget. To clean up their minds. The discipline of the body and the recourse to alcohol meeting up as the two opposite ends of the same quest.

Very few moments of intimacy slip out of everyone's participation in the everyday life of the cycling nation and even the callings of love sometimes turn into team performances. Sex is also a stage in which they see themselves through the eyes of their peers as much as in the eyes of their partners and as a result, when they do not simply boast about them, they never keep their affairs secret. Podium girls, who travel as much as they do, or local beauty queens find themselves seduced or abused, adding love groans to the fantasy life of the monster. But most of the time, as they rest their skinny, livid, almost child-like chests between fresh sheets, they are alone.

9

Grace and Disgrace

On the stage of his inner theater, the rider, like all of us, plays several parts. He pretends to be studying sometimes, he has loved women and even his wife and children, he poses as a reader and sits at small tables, his back bent in front of a computer. But he cannot fool himself. When he sets his elbows solidly on each side of a book he struggles to understand and takes his head in his hands, he cannot completely fend off the impression that he is leaning on the handlebars to go faster. He feels the wind slide over his shoulders, even between four walls. He cannot walk up stairs, step by step or two by two, without the obsessive thought of a change of gear or cadence. He could admit to many other guilty ideas when each move he makes reminds him incongruously of some riding situation. Maybe he always acts hoping for a bunch of flowers. Whatever his occupation, the rider inside is always liable to influence his daily gestures.

It could be said that he dedicated so much time and energy to that particular type of effort that the rider's disposition has taken over the rest. So much time and energy indeed. Yet it is difficult to estimate the amount of that furious expense. It can of course be judged by the production of mechanical energy, following the canon law of contemporary sport, and be expressed in abstract form as the balance between two types of measures, the duration of effort and mechanical power. But it would reduce to a few features and a limited symbolic principle the infinite richness of expressions on a rider's face. Effort in this case is as easily recognizable as Marxist ideas on a Che Guevara T-shirt.

Performance, even if we try to simplify it into the production of a finely calibrated movement, cannot be produced by a machine; it implies a person, therefore a changing principle that cannot be measured. To be approached in all its truth and its depth, performance requires something else, a portrait or at least a form of contemplation. Storytelling is probably the right method in this instance.

So this is summer and so this is the Tour de France. The television images of the race are part of the collective unconscious so that everybody can picture, in their own way, what an "escapee" looks like. Most of the time, we imagine him in the spectacular setting of a mountain landscape, tackling a merciless climb and ignoring his own pain. We could give him the features and outlook of Frenchman Thomas Voeckler, brave in his suffering, his jersey wide open and riding in a rather uncomfortable style, full of impatience and impetus. Or opt for the unfailing elegance of Alberto Contador and think of his stroke of the pedal, as sharp as a saber, his feet turning like the luminous blades of a lighthouse slicing through the night, remembering his ride on the slopes of Etna in 2011.

After the first shady turns, generally scarcely crowded, the coolness and the calm are suddenly taken away from him when the trees vanish and he comes out in the blinding sun of July, where the cheers fall on his back with more and more intensity. Soon he is overheating. As in the ascent of the previous passes, he sweats heavily and he knows (but it is a thought that he sweeps out of his mind with a shiver like many others) that at the shade of that small house of bricks on the left, his eyelids will be covered with salt. Motorbikes are opening the way, digging a brief crack in the flood of people now rushing toward him and, as much as it can, a camera is alternately licking his legs and his face. The vision comes to him of his contorted mask all over the TV screen—don't think about it. He spits, wipes his face with the back of his glove, looks down at his feet, stands up—and his strutting chest plunges again in the tide of grimaces and screams wrapping around him, hardly protected by the prow of the motorcyclists ahead of him. He focuses on his pace in a deafening racket of voices and colors. That's it for the show.

Yet the noise scarcely affects him—otherwise he would be carried away and the nice unity of his movements would be shattered.

In a way, everything is foreign to him, because what he works on is not so much the space around him as the essentially inner space defined by the dimensions of his bike and the posture it imposes on him. It could be put in a different and even opposite way, by considering that nothing is foreign to him and that he turns the physical space into an inner space. All the elements of the landscape are taken with him in an isolating power that disjoints and multiplies the world. Nevertheless, from the spectator's point of view, pedaling is seldom seen as a form of gesticulation. And all the visible space, the limited visible space inside of which he moves, wraps him up like a vibrating aura that he carries along with him on the ribbon of the road.

For the rider, it is a question of rhythm, or even rhythms. He must adjust everything, the breathing, the blood, the flesh, to his aims and his craving for speed. The pulse, the lungs, the cadence of his beaming knees moving up and down. Yet all these organs, and the infinite population of cells flocking in his body, and the colonies of bacteria inherited from the family tree, all those things that he pretends to be managing are actually ready to blow apart in conflicting and obscure projects.

Everything is against him, not totally, not frontally, not as a complete negation of his intentions, but everything is in contention: he needs to listen to all those voices and pacify all those conflicts. Everything is against him and yet it is thanks to that extreme tension, thanks to the vibrating resistance, he tames, transforms, and assimilates that he exists. He attracts those discording voices, seduces, gathers, and convinces them easily at first. For he does not fool himself: from his hierarchical position at the top, he will not prevent anything from existing for its own sake. The only thing he wants is to ride fast. To ride from one turn to the next on that road that you can no longer see. To keep his rivals at bay, fearing more than anything else the smell of their breath upon his back. For now, he can do it. The air that whistles in his lungs, that he pushes as deeply as he can inside the bronchial tube, will eventually blow through him. His neck and shoulders are relaxed, he can feel the power of his legs, from his kidneys to his toes, spray a burning syrup in the thick of his muscles and spread under his skin shiny colors of oil paint. Everything is fine. He can maintain the pace. He enjoys it while it lasts. No evil thought gets in the way, nothing is tempting him or suggesting that he should quit. His own weight on the slope, the mechanical resistance of the pedal, he takes care of them. His physical existence is finely tuned with the images going through his eyes and the feelings swelling his tongue. It melts into them.

He lives, like every time he rides and tries to ride fast, inside himself. That is betrayed by the frequent moments when he curls up, when he looks down. What he is mimicking then is a posture that would allow his eyes to see inside himself. With each contraction of the muscles, it seems as though under his pedals and his wheels a cavity is opening, to which he would love to give the dimensions of a cathedral. While he digs that dark hole, he peers into it as well, knowing that other intentions than his own are lurking, with which he will soon be forced to negotiate.

Pushing down the pedals, he kicks behind him the tarmac and time. He sees his feet turning like perfect satellites in their nice shoes (he loves his shoes); he enjoys feeling them as much as watching them. He is on the edge, on the sharp top of his effort. He stands at the right distance, adapting the right approach to the right resistance. His pain? He has dodged it and fended it off like a bullfighter. It swells, sweats, roars, you can barely hear it and it charges in a fetid breath, threatens to gore him. But with a discreet motion, he dodges it and it vanishes inside the far depths of his stomach. He could almost stroke its sweaty skin as it passes by. As for suffering on a bicycle, believe me, he knows it all too well. He is not a beginner: he knows the conflicting mass inside him, he knows its weight and its menace, he knows how it can come out of the dark. He is like the famous bullfighter Juan Belmonte, who would stand alone at night in a field at the mercy of a bull: to succeed, he needs a sharp attention, a kind of hearing applied to the entire internal surface of the skin. He listens in the dark, carefully waiting for the pounding of the animal's hooves on the ground. Anticipating, looking forward to it, staying absolutely, supernaturally calm. *Festina lente.* Keeping the momentum, making it last, means being able to not "enter into the red zone." It requires several subtle swerves, carefully rehearsed passes, a special disposition to ride beside your pain, to ride along with it without letting it take you away. To let the pain pass in the end. Pass and pass again, without letting it get the best of you.

So the rider stands up. He dances internally. When he rides past you in a flash it lasts only a second, and the flickering of his eyelids is what strikes you the most. He is still light and lively. He ignores his pain, he avoids it, he turns it down, eludes it. He fools it. He moves along with it every time it comes too close, he lies to it. He moves it around, too: that is why he bites his tongue. A drop of blood to rush for, to take the pain to a part of the body where it cannot do any damage.

And the minutes pass. The top of the pass is nearing and might see him win in the bulging glass eye of the camera, on the television screens, those inverted retinas.

He is on top of his game because he is no longer his own boss. It is as though the harmony he created with the might of his will was now replacing him. He is like the zen archers, who worked so hard to let "something inside of them shoot in their place." He is his own spectator and he enjoys the show. Something has broken and he is spurred by that something else he has been praying for with all his soul, that he has aroused with all his strength. He is no longer on the deciding end, he feels like the tension itself, he dances on the tightrope, above time. Always the same little flashes of eternity. It comes to him open-handed, he recognizes it and names it immediately: grace, that is what it is.

But then a certain disorder takes place. While every rotation of the legs was merging with the previous one, identical, a slight limp has taken over and the white-hot moves are cooling down. Here and there, oddly, a stroke of the pedal follows another, slightly out of tune. A sudden malaise creeps in, like a hand on the back of the neck, moves down to the shoulders and to the arms, which are no longer as smooth as though strangled by a tie. His hands grope along the handlebars. He changes his grip a few times. Stands up, sits back, and each time more briskly. He literally falls apart. He is no longer one but a combination of parts. He swings around and time stretches again on the horizon.

Grace and Disgrace

And then he recognizes that pain has abused him. It has gored him for good this time. It is already shaking him around like a puppet on the sand where it is about to throw him down as his blood starts pouring.

He is determined to keep fighting. The thing that had taken his place and was riding on his behalf is rejecting him now and he tries to adapt to the new demands of the situation. He asks himself questions, he now needs to put words to what is happening to him and he finds himself speaking in the first person again.

But he is no longer running the show. He can only address that block of indistinct strangeness that invaded his effort and look for someone to talk to. Like a dictator about to be overthrown, for he now has to cope with open conflict, he tries to play it smart, to charm once more. Out of anguish, he outrageously flatters even the lowest and most miserable elements of the organization he thought he was controlling. His head, swept by the wind, shaken by the chemistry of blood, hypoglycemia, and hormones, does not control anything anymore. Through the mechanical eye of the camera, as you keep watching him, you might sense the amount of life he is trying to instill in his body and his posture. He sneezes and his beautiful eyes, once pure and still, jump around now, unable to fix on anything as though everything they look at is turning away. He sneezes, wipes his nose on his elbow. Thick spit underlines the corners of his mouth; salt, as he feared it would, clots on his skin, and if you move closer you will notice his hair standing on end and his complexion going pale. He becomes another and his body is the other of the other and is no longer itself, and everything is embedded and, indeed, threatens to collapse.

In a few minutes, the casting changes: his chasers rein him in and drop him. Not only will he not win but he now progresses slowly, he grips awkwardly to the climb, and the stunned stuttering of his legs inspires only heaviness and powerlessness. His disgrace is as immeasurable as the marvelous blossoming it replaced. But he is no longer worth much in this world where everything dies, and he would probably give anything to stare once again at that place where everything is pure and blue, beyond the clouds of flesh and gravity.

10

Go to Heaven with Your Body

What they are actually chasing so breathlessly is their own death. It is the secret behind the blank expression in their eyes. Fighting their way through the scrum, they are clinging to the heels of the Reaper. They are a frightening sight to see. They rode up from the valley with the muffled rumble surrounding them. Now they are moving up the slope at a prodigious speed, their arms spread around the steely hammering of their knees, their tormented faces turned toward the summit. Through their open jerseys, the dreadful spider of their ribs and breastbone swells and hisses and their wheels slide over the remains of their names smudged across the tarmac.

Those luminous bodies, those creatures we watch as they dissolve their earthly sheaths in the bath of their desire, are conventionally seen as bad boys. Not by me. I could not care less about the bursts of indignation they spur in many a mouth, especially when that criticism comes after effusive commentaries on the show, flourished by the clichés pulled from the common box of praises. The evidence of their mystification, brandished in front of the crowd like the skull of a hanged man, leaves me cold.

They have long lived in hiding. Nights after the race, they would lock themselves up in their room with some mysterious equipment. In the lobbies, others were watching. We could only imagine what was going on behind those closed doors, in those silent spaces covered with velvet hangings, wavering from scarlet to purple in the candlelight. Trembling shadows reflecting the uneasy breathing of excitement. They would lie down, pale under hanging vermilion bags, a tiny hose stuck in their arm, until night fell. The next day, blushing from their refreshed blood, they would clip their shoes into the pedals, confident that they would no longer falter and that they would display the best of their talent all day. Yet—rays of light under the door, whispers and whines surely not due to lovemaking—some mentioned insomnias and nightly activities. The inhuman blood, they said, imposed its own punishment, as if death were hanging over their sleep. Thick, viscous, that mash of red cells was hampering the circulation in their lungs, embolism was looming and forcing them to sleep in short fractions mixed with exercise.

Since then, many synthetic wonders have been dangled in front of those werewolves. You keep dreaming about fabulous animals. They say there were attempts to reproduce archaic hemoglobin like that of the sperm whale, which releases in the tissues the four oxygen atoms it carries.

Who knows?

But the fact that professional cyclists struggle to resist the temptations of those scary enhancing manipulations and even that they are often quite ready to use them is also what makes them fascinating. I find their incredible disdain for their own health moving. It pleads in favor of what they should be forgiven for. Basically, it is total innocence. Cyclists do not dope out of calculation or to make a career: those reasons only come afterward. They dope gratuitously, they do it because it is good. Because to ride that fast is such a wonderful experience that it makes caution irrelevant. Such a great experience that you would give your life to go through it again. That is what I forgive them for and even what makes them so pure in my opinion. They are only looking for another taste of singular delights. Nothing was planned. After their first rides, they went from surprise to surprise. Whatever you may think of early vocations, none of these riders had any idea of what was awaiting them. You can dream of results, and work for them, but that is not yet living them.

Go to Heaven with Your Body

The way to the top is splattered with wonders: you never knew you could ride that climb so fast, use those gears, but above all you feel the unspeakable sensation of a body with limitless powers and you sometimes have the undefinable impression that you can reach a sort of disembodied life.

It is because they are from time to time dazzled by themselves that they turned into those Dionysiac monsters, always ready to eat out their own guts, worn out not so much by their years of asceticism but by their vertiginous fascination for the eternity of the moment.

The most poorly paid riders do not dope less than the wealthiest. There is no misery in ecstasy. I was in my best years a mediocre rider and I was hardly making a penny and yet I experienced the terrible pleasure and the odd muscular eloquence of amphetamines. I was dreaming for them to emulate my best days. Those wonderful moments when I managed to sprint fifty or sixty times up the same climb without any harm but the progressive and controlled increase of muscular pain. Those times when I could ride all day without weariness or boredom and adapt easily to the pace set by others. Those days when I was not cold, not hot, not hungry, when the disappearance of need turned into an enormous pleasure and when the only mark on the flesh was a succession of images in my brain. Thanks to amphetamines, I was bringing back those scarce moments of grace that reward, let's face it, the work of every dedicated and sincere rider. Those moments when I had looked down in bewilderment at my arms and legs, at my whole body, as if trying to make sure they were there or to check the reason why everyone was looking at me uncomfortably. And if they led me, when I finally gave up racing, to a kind of exhaustion of the soul, administered daily, it was because I could no longer stand the burden of my body. Because I wanted to feel once more the inexpressible feeling of pure exhaustion. The wish to become but an ember in a draft and burn out.

Unaware of the formula and because they strive desperately every day in that gap, those experienced human beings know better than most that "man is crippled by his distance from the world." When they have the impression, even just once, that they have abolished that distance, they are lost. Possessed, mystics, using all the means available in their time, they drag their body into that impossible adventure that can lead only to heaven. "Violence and endless suffering are the lot of the men who want to go to heaven with their body," wrote monk John Climacus, author of *La Scala Paradisi*. What can be less evil than such a leaning toward grace?

While I'm quite partial to those reviled men, I'm not totally unaware that some of them are or were contemptible characters, systematically sullied by the traits I personally find unacceptable: narcissistic, sadistic, manipulative, selfish, violent. Obviously, it does not apply to all of them, far from it.

I keep watching with fondness some moments of cycling in the 1990s, a period considered by the official dogma (a little quickly to my taste) as the darkest era in the sport's history. For I cannot see what sort of disaster made it possible to justify Fausto Coppi's mystical melancholy, Jacques Anquetil's elegant cynicism, or the suicidal obstinacy of the first "convicts of the road," high on wine or cocaine, while denying the feats of the champions of that recent period any spiritual dimension.

In their wool jerseys and on their steel bicycles weighing ten kilos, the men were not so very different from what they are today in their impeccable outfits. The number of cogs went from five for Anquetil to seven or eight for Hinault and to eleven today. The whole environment of the race has changed. The quality of the tarmac is probably better, there are fewer ruts hence fewer crashes. The riders are better and more systematically trained. And there are fewer wooden shelves and china pots in the shops of chemists. But beneath the layers of technology and make-believe, under the bark of circumstances and culture, still radiates the inalterable hard core that needs to be exposed and always relates to effort. It is important, if one wishes to appreciate cycling races, to extract that beating heart from the shell and contemplate the talent that owes nothing to the mechanical life of the organs.

Yet what is happening beneath the visible film, what the light does not reveal, is not out of reach. Between the movements and the moments, behind the muscles and the whole organic set-up, the peculiar presence of the men still vibrates along with ours, full of memories, fears, and images (in which our own figure sometimes appears in a glimpse if we were there). What should be considered as the performance of a rider is the unreachable picture of conscience, of which we can still guess the main outlines, the main shades and lights. The show he attempts to transform, to reshuffle by enhancing one aspect while blurring another by the sole action of his motricity is what we should bear in mind to judge the beauty of the ride. To try and identify that form of conscience is hazardous, I agree. But it is the way to go.

On screen I again watch Lance Armstrong, whose arrogance and cruelty I believe were unique, riding the climbs of the Tour de France. The amazing speed at which his flayed figure flies past the concrete pillars of the avalanche barriers of La Mongie, his iliopsoas pulling the knees so high and violently that they seem about to be torn apart from his lower back; his sunken cheeks and his wide eyes ringed with purple and lemon as he thrashes ahead after crashing heavily because of a spectator in Luz Ardiden. We know that he is doped, but it is not the point. Armstrong is a madman. Like all the riders of his rank before and after him, what is at stake is his very existence. He is mad, I said: the role he is playing is the fable of Acteon, an Ovidian myth rejuvenated by Giordano Bruno in his *Heroic Frenzies*. Acteon, who went hunting with his hounds, comes upon Diana, who is taking a bath. Having seen what no mortal should see, he is cruelly punished by the goddess, who turns him into a deer and lets him be devoured by his own dogs. Yet the violent outcome is not so dire: Acteon could not have hoped for a better ending since, by becoming the very prey he was hunting, he does much more than reaching it and killing it.

In other words, thanks to his desire to know, Acteon sought and found an ecstatic experience. One tends to forget that this quest for surpassing oneself is precisely what is expected of an athlete. Acteon performs, which literally means that he goes across his own form, through it, and transforms in order to conform with the prey he was aiming at. A mad rider is almost a dead man, who only bids to forget himself for the benefit of his feat, to erase the outlines and the sketches of his body for the sake of the movement, to dissolve his individual limits into the very process and the achievement of his transformation.

That is what Armstrong was after in his madness, and

so are all the dopers (since we have to indulge in using such a miserable word). When, during his first Tour de France victory in 1999, he won the stage to Sestriere (now considered the symbol of the Armstrong mystification), unexpectedly because until then he had never been seen as a climber, his emaciated face led to talk of him as a "cancer survivor" (which he was). Personally, I maintain that I saw a dead man on the finish line that day.

As for Frank Vandenbroucke, another one of the notorious mavericks in my personal hall of fame, when he grabbed his handlebars by the middle to tackle (or should I say *fuck,* which would be more accurate) the nearly twenty percent of the Côte de la Redoute to pin down Michele Bartoli, his rival, like an owl to the door of a barn, I could identify the mute, divine, and crazy hope that verges on the cancellation of the self or at least demands to *take all the risks.* That is why cycle racing has been so fascinating for so long—because it is the work of men who leave their very skin on the table, because what they are seeking is priceless. They are injured, knackered huntsmen whose transformation has started but will never be completed. The exact opposite of the pleasant and respectable man that I am trying to be as much as I can, knowing, as I watch my children sleep, that only the lack of talent prevented me from becoming one of those huntsmen.

It is interesting and not too difficult to make the imaginary experience of a cycling race without the madness and the fury, whose actors would be reasonable and would not attempt to surpass themselves but would stay within their limits. It seems to me that such an event, while not entirely pointless, would have little in common with what we expect from convicts. Would we wait all day, our ear glued to the wireless, would we camp in packs several days in advance on the rocky roadside of a mountain pass to see and *feel* circumspect and moderate athletes, carefully protecting their bourgeois health and stopping their efforts to not test themselves too far?

Beneath the hard and matte varnish of seemliness and prudishness, layers of which have been applied to it lately, the heart of cycle racing, which is essentially foolish and outrageous, survives more than it beats to its own spasms. Otherwise it might have vaguely aroused a glimmer of interest in the eyes of the most reasonable, the most aloof of us, but it would not have fascinated and moved the crowds the way it did. The problem with reason is that it can only overflow and betray itself in order to achieve greatness—and if cycling champions were great, it was because they were crazy. I sincerely hope they still are. This warning from playwright Tristan Bernard, who also was the director of a cycling track, comes to mind: "Never mess around with cyclists, they put the world at risk every five hundred meters." The tragic masks that did so much for the iconic memory of the sport reflect nothing less than the serenity of calculation. Champions are gutted and bitten by a peculiar form of gloom and hope: they are trying to find one more time the grace that, once in a while and too rarely, struck them. To open wide the door through which they caught a glimpse of light. Or, if you remember St. Thomas's finger stuck in the open womb in the side of Christ, to ride straight into the Kingdom. Compared to this, what is the earthly life worth? Can they devote to their art only a small portion of their time, like going to church on a Sunday morning before returning to the daily and predictable turpitudes of your lives? What is the bucket mentioned by Jean Giono, in which you are supposed to "clean your soul" to avoid having to carry "such litter in a golden vase when you are so obsessed with cleanliness"?

Think of Padre Pio. Once slashed by the sharp blades of divine light, how could he renounce the bloody cuts that related him to Christ and how could he be blamed, as some gossipers did, for using acid to retain his stigmata?

11

Nocturne

Night does not calm them down. Far from it. You even wonder.

In the hot season, when the major races do not want them, second-tier riders sometimes make a bit of money. They put their bike and their bag in their car and go on tour. Their life is a circus. Along the way, they sometimes provide some entertainment for vacationers.

You can see them ride in circles with their colleagues with the damp skin of a summer night in the background. The small trips allowed by spare time are none of their business. Picture a street on which they sprint tirelessly, alone in their world, as usual. A street swarming with chairs and crossed legs, with packed terraces under the garlands, with crippled plane trees and mossy fountains littered with hard luck and small coins. They will ride sixty or a hundred times past the same spots, in front of the same tourists, or the same empty glasses, on the brink of a more peaceful world than the one they live in, flowing with ordinary weariness. They ride around the area like butterflies around a lamp, briefly turned away from their course by an occasional burn.

They come from one side, rush like a wave onto the square where the finish line is painted and where the podium bus is parked, a kind of empty shell where the speaker seems to live all year round and from which he listens to his own metallic echo. Then they ride along the entire street in the light and outbursts. They keep silent and for now work hard without a moan or a word. They dance, both hands on the handlebars. They hurry. As if in a rush, but nothing more. Further up the road, light spills through the glass doors and down the stairs of an old movie theater. Their leaning backs are lit a last time by the red shades of the neon signs before vanishing on the right, in the descent at the corner of the post office. Unless the cinema is at the bottom of the brief slope and the post office at the top. They don't really care. They ride on. They lean a hundred times into the same bend, a hundred times they emerge at the brink of the curb, their two wheels in the ditch. Now they dive into that dark and deserted lane, slightly lopsided but their mouths open wide, full gas, the whole bunch stretched in the newly found rectitude like a cable uncoiled by the weight of an anchor. Almost as soon as the hissing of the pedals has stopped in that long turn in which they did not use their brakes, as soon as the clicking of chains, echoed by the dark walls as they moved up a gear, has faded, they are back already. Spectators stretch their necks as if on the side of a tennis court, following a leading bunch for a few meters before turning back again to welcome the long muffled scream of the peloton spreading along the whole extent of their cervical range. A good hundred riders always riding in the same direction, throwing themselves on the same three or four roads all night long, on the same mile-long circuit, hardly leaves enough time to do a few steps or sip a drink calmly. And then, after a few laps, when the race starts moving ahead, the snake will begin to eat its tail and the eyes of the crowd will become totally restless, fascinated as if by a swarm of locusts. They call that kind of race through town (and there is always someone on the side of the circuit to utter the word) a "tourniquet," French for "merry-go-round" and not for "tourniquet"!

You can go for a stroll and walk along with them. Turn to the left and backward, but to see things from their point of view it is better to walk in the same direction and discover the whole of the circuit. Rub your eyelids a couple of times. Walk up the street to the above-mentioned cinema and turn back from time to time to see them from the front and stick names to the binary roars coming toward you, to the bifid shins, tight as ropes, pulling on those skinny shoulders. The cinema is a little bit further up and you see them from afar pulling up short into the bend. The brakes shriek on the carbon rims. The stars of flesh turn into comets. Breathless at the top of the small hill, they pull aside one after the other, suddenly leaving their orbit as though all the air to breathe was on the sides, and then they dive to the other end of the road and into the long descending curve. Their backs lean forward one by one like dominoes or majorettes. They are pouring down.

After a few laps, behind the two forerunners on their motorbikes, the leading riders are always the same. Bored with screwing up your head every hundred meters and with walking sideways to see them coming, you decide to take a break and you stand still, legs apart, on the edge of the pavement. You are at the top of the hill. A few meters before the turn, a vital pocket of fresh air seems to open up where they come to breathe before diving again into the slope and you see them like dolphins on their way to the deep sea. It looks as though, with a slight motion of the head, they come and leave there on the roadside the result of long seconds of breathlessness.

One rider is more active, more vehement than the rest. No need to be an expert to notice it. He is very agitated. With almost every lap, he reaches the top ahead of his companions, looks swiftly behind him, tilted on a stretched leg, in a kind of *contrapposto,* the torsion of the chest enhanced by the jutting elbow. Behind him, a muffled whine resounds, coming from the very flesh of the serpentine body. The battle claims its first casualties. The flood carries a small collection of bleak and panicky faces, floating atop the roaring stream that will soon take them under. That big and virulent rider, who seems to hurt the whole pack on his own, is not the most elegant. His shoulders move up and down, he stretches his arms and pulls them back together. From a group of young women and their cheers, we learn that his first name is Ludo, for example. *Come on, Ludo!* The support is shouted in a firm voice but without excitement or emotion. From the way they cheer without overdoing it, you can guess that those young women who all know each other are the partners, the girlfriends, the wives of the riders. As a matter of fact, they will soon step ahead on the tarmac, their arms outstretched, a bottle of water in their hands. The big Ludo will grab his without a word or a glance at his sweetheart. He pinches the bridge of his nose as he rides past and quickly blows his nostrils before throwing himself mechanically into the corner and further down in the dark. The skin of his thin legs, scarred with veins reflected by the neon lights. The small bit of drool at the corner of his lips. Ludo is not the most elegant but he is damned efficient.

Succession and repetition have their toll. Sprint on the finish line, where bonuses are awarded, climb, braking, turn, descent, brakeless corner, long full-gas open-mouthed stretch, more corners, and the finish line. Light, shadow, light. A group gradually parts from the tormented peloton. Ludo, of course, and three other guys along with him. Four men, "the leading four," as the commentator calls them predictably in the loudspeakers hanging from the posts. Next to the overactive Ludo, two other riders, smart and collected, are going easily and seem to be in total control—they stare straight ahead and sometimes look back calmly, gauging the situation as they would estimate the value of property. Despite the hellish pace (judging by the tragic masks now covering the rest of the faces), they reposition themselves effortlessly, almost carelessly, in the slipstream of the group after taking their turn. These men are of a noble breed. As for the fourth guy, seen with a bit of experience, he is not in such a good position. Visibly harmed by Ludo's fury and by the stylish arrogance of the two regents, he hangs on as best he can.

The script is always the same in the kind of races that riders use to make ends meet. They team up to snatch as much of the prizes given away with each lap as they can. The partners do not attack each other and they share their earnings at the end, each one pocketing the same amount. The local rider, if he is good enough to keep the tempo, is often spontaneously involved in the joint venture: he will give his share to the others to be allowed to win. You can be a prophet in your homeland when necessary.

You can hardly see a thing in the long, poorly lit stretch

leading back to the finish line. For the occasion, local authorities have removed the last parked cars, revealing stains of oil and petrol on the tarmac. Backyard feelings. Passersby so scarce they might be threatening. Muffled showers of lights intermittently displayed by worn-out lampposts. The riders descend in their silent fury. Sounds of tires, of chains changing gear, puffs, spits, and brief moans. Their colorful figures emerge one by one in the beams, singled out in flashes before vanishing again. Ludo embodies the rider's ecstasy, lying between his folded elbows, at full speed. From one cone of light to the next, he plays with the ghost of his shadow, which he sees come up to him, hide away and grow, wiggle its hips and jump at his face, an explosion of pitch-black night before a new, immediate dawn.

The four leading backs increase their lead on the peloton that sent them up front. Exchange a few brief words, negotiate. Will you? Say what you think. Make up your mind. Come on. And once again, they surge in the floodlights and the metallic voice: two hundred euros from the Banette bakery. In big Ludo's bag. Riders are more often proles than pros, but a touch of romanticism improves their everyday fare.

A few more laps and it will be over. You leave the table, you elbow your way along the narrow pavement, through the meager crowd and behind the metal barriers. If you find the right spot, you stick a foot between the bars to watch a few sprints and then the finale.

Now comes the shocker. The rider leading the way by a few seconds over the other three is not Ludo. It is precisely the one on whom, given the odds, nobody would have bet a penny.

And he indeed displays all the features of pain. His jaws quartered, his tongue sticking out, deep wrinkles at the corner of his eyes, his flesh shiny, he braces on his bandaged legs. But it makes him oddly beautiful, as if he had burnt down his limits and all the angles of his body. From his open mouth pour out the images he still plays back inside his head. His cranium at that very moment must look like the ceiling of a Renaissance nuptial bedroom, painted with bloody allegories, a mess of clouds and anger. You would swear he can no longer breathe. He feels, and is desperate about it because he would love to ride even faster, the small warm ball of suffocation swell deep inside his guts. He would love to get rid of it, make it come up, throw it up, but there is nothing he can do, it knocks on his plexus. Breath is a small animal that you cannot spit out.

The line crossed, a few meters further up or in the adjacent streets, sitting on the frame of their bikes, a towel around their necks, they down a few cans of water or soda, they cough and they spit on the sides one last time. After rinsing their ribs and armpits, after rubbing their dirty legs with cologne or Synthol, they go to the podium bus to pick their flowers or their cup. The casquette is compulsory. They then look for the village hall, where an official hands out their fares and their bonuses in envelopes bearing the number on their bib. They spread their shoulders against the back of a chair, shake up their T-shirt with the manners of a duke, like you would a fan. Still sweating, they yawn endlessly and sometimes keep gulping under the influence of some powerful stimulant.

When finally, after picking up their envelopes, they return to the dark through the door, the partners in crime of the day tackle the accounting process. In a corner, under layers of shade and orange light, they settle their accounts. Afterward, each one of them in his car and in his own night, hands calmly trembling on the steering wheel, they head toward an unlikely night of sleep and the next day's race.

12

Physique

You find in the peloton all sorts of builds, each one more suited to a role and a terrain—climbers weighing eighty kilos are as rare and odd as sixty-kilo *rouleurs*. The only specialty recruiting in every weight category is sprint, even though sprinters are almost always unable to "climb a railway bridge" because their musculature is not adapted to climbing. But from the 1.88 meters of Marcel Kittel to the 1.65 meters of Caleb Ewan to the 1.75 meters of Mark Cavendish, the fastest finishers on the planet make up a disparate photo-finish. And although on the scales and on the measuring rod (a difference of two centimeters and three kilos), Nairo Quintana, the climber, and Caleb Ewan, the sprinter, are pretty close, their competences are entirely opposite.

The first degree on the scale of humility for the rider is to accept himself as he is and to consider personal qualities as his "natural register." If there is something that riders have in common with opera singers it is that they reflect Freud's famous saying that "anatomy is destiny."

Yet, a way of life that devotes three to six hours daily to muscular strain and breathlessness tends to carve the body one way or another and can lead to spectacular transformations. There is the story of an overweight young man who, in the darkness of his family home in the suburbs of Lucerne, lost nearly sixty kilos in a few months without leaving his room, starving himself for four to eight hours a day on an exercise bike. When I saw that monument of rust (can you imagine how much you sweat by pedaling from dawn until sunset?), finally out of order, it was still standing in the middle of an attic paneled with pine. A big boombox was on a table, within reach of the rider. With a finger, unintentionally, I pressed a flaky (sweat again) red switch and the screams of a saturated guitar burst through the room.

What image of time and self you must have to pedal all day by swallowing a few apples as your only food and by simply opening up your mind through a Lucerne FM heavy-metal radio station, I don't know. But in that archaeological process seeking to unearth his buried body, in that kind of self-parturition, the ascetic young man discovered he had serious aerobic capacities. Coming out of his strange purgatory and strengthened by such a disposition to loneliness, a cyclist was born. He quite successfully turned to time trials and track records and found a job. He was a pro rider for five or six years before being sacked. He did not leave much of a trace in the pelotons he was joining in almost perfect silence.

There is a transformation that was as famous as Jean Nuttli's metamorphosis was discreet. The mutation of Lance Armstrong, whom nobody (except Cyrille Guimard and Eddy Merckx) saw as a potential Tour de France champion, or even a stage race winner, before he came close to dying from cancer. And who won the Tour seven times after his remission before a court decision purely and simply deleted his record for doping practices.

It is notorious that the young Texan's range, as gifted as he was (he won the world championship at the age of twenty-one), was strictly limited to one-day races and flat terrain but not, absolutely not, to the mountains. You cannot call "climbing," when you are a professional rider, hills of one or two kilometers: those ascents require between two and four minutes of effort, and even the bulky ones are excellent on them. However, beyond that distance and duration, "bumps" require specific energy systems, and above all a power-to-weight ratio favorable for slopes. To keep it simple, you must be light. Even more so in the high Alpine passes, which only crown featherweights or the rare members of a kind of physiological jet set capable of recycling phenomenal quantities of oxygen. Lance

Physique

Armstrong looked too robustly built for that, and his first Tours de France saw him win a stage here and there, but in the mountains he would systematically finish with the last groups. We know that disease changed him. Or that he took the opportunity of disease (he suffered from advanced testicular cancer) to change. As to how much weight he lost in the process, stories are conflicting. But his physical appearance was definitely disrupted: whatever the verdict of the scales, you needed only eyes to notice it. His muscular and square frame turned from thick to skinny and also became more fluid and sketchy. What is odd is the silent acceptance that took place around the idea that his body had changed—allegations amply circulated about a secret and exceptional chemotherapy cure—but he had not. In any case, his soul was never mentioned, as if the evils he has since been accused of, more or less rightly, were disqualifying him as an animated person.

So what did Armstrong do with his soul in the mephitic and miraculous vapors of the chemotherapy from which he emerged cured, healed, and restored to the point of dominating a race he never could have fancied to win? Possibility of a body nourished and built in a peculiar bath of loving emotion? Virtues of self-discovery through disease? The episode evokes the model of the Faustian pact or the mysteries of shamanic transmission. The legend of bluesman Robert Johnson, once a mediocre and suddenly a fabulous guitar player after a disappearance of a few days, comes to mind. Or a kind of purely physical conversion, finally not more unlikely than the sudden shifts of the soul. It is absurd, or at least superficial, to see such a metamorphosis only as the result of a series of biological or chemical treatments. If athletic asceticism is definitely a "practice" or "an enhancement of the self through exercise," as was the spiritual dimension of the ancient physical exercises, it is because you cannot remain exactly the same through the upheavals of the flesh.

Cyclists see their bodies in a very peculiar way. You could be tempted to say that they take care of it with violence, like a talisman from which they magically expect everything, and that they hate because they cannot break free from it. The more they hunt down extra weight for very practical reasons, the more they take a real and wicked pleasure at the sight of their skinny selves. Among those emaciated Narcissi, the most impressive are the professionals, of course. They are frequently skeletal, which gives them a shivering and uncertain aura, like the flame of a candle displaying around as much shade as light. Their presence radiates with dazzling form and the dark fragility of crystal. Their skin is never fine or transparent enough for their taste. They pinch it to separate it from the muscles and roll it between their fingers, an oddly and vaguely culinary gesture. As for the "sharpest" of them, you could nearly stick a finger between their ribs; you would be surprised to find out that their breastbone sticks out of their scrawny chest. From head to toe, they are covered with an ivy of veins (the more swollen as they are tired or dehydrated) of which they are really proud.

Honestly, in those days you could see my veins down to my buttocks.

The total absence of hair makes their epidermis even more translucid and they look like porn stars or anatomic charts.

Perhaps, by the odd principle of coincidence of the opposites that they often inspire in those who look for words to describe them, they have crossed to the other side of what made them young and beautiful. It is always dangerous at the top. But to the spells of narcissistic love that blind and graze them can be added a more harmless anecdotal disposition. They sport their spectacular tan lines with such convincing pride that they turn what should make them a laughing-stock into something desirable. Naked in front of their sex partners, they parade in that two-tone outfit as if playing with the shadows and light reflecting off the ceiling. The back-to-back juxtaposition of the surfaces of white and burnt skin turns into the emblem of their heroic existence, the evidence of their exposure to danger and of their commitment to their colors. And it would be necessary, in order to get the full picture, to add to the list of their traits the heraldic aspect of their battle scars, these medals spread and disposed on their hips, elbows, and knees like chivalric blazons or purple hearts.

Ignoring the warning made to Narcissus ("he will live if he does not know himself"), they let themselves be contaminated by the fascinated looks they attract and turn restlessly around their own statue of flesh, raising a cuddling or hostile hand in its direction. They look after themselves like enlightened drunks, better and more often than is commonly thought, following vague prescriptions regarding the heart, the liver, or the intestine, which they consider personal entities. At the cold (and alleged) dawn of genetic doping, folk remedies are still an important part of their daily life and they can still be seen boiling aspirin in Coke.

While it is often said that few disciplines leave the body as bare as cycling, it is not only a reference to the rider's thin and skin-tight outfit. It is not so much because they are cold or hot or because, when they crash, nothing protects them from abrasion and they leave more than skin on the ground. If they are bare, it is because the duration and frequency of races turn their discipline into an imitation of life. A daily routine on two wheels—that is what they feel when they race. Those men have changed bodies and now live on a bike: we said it before, even though they do not sleep in the bunch, they lunch in it, they live as a society, they sometimes dress or undress in it. They think within the peloton, they hope in it, lose that hope and get it back. There are very, very few races whose winner, between start and finish, has not gone through moments of doubt and despondency. Distress is a must in cycling races. The few examples of total control and absolute domination should not fool you. It is extremely rare that a rider knows what he is doing from the first to the last kilometer—not even Peter Sagan. Cycling requires a dose of stoicism. Even in your best form, racing can throw you each day into myriads of miseries, big or small. To shit yourself, literally, without a chance of giving up or stopping, is what happened to Jan Ullrich on the Tour de France. Because of effort, a descent in the rain, or too cold a drink. To tackle the last climb and sometimes find new strength, to focus on your pedaling and ride through the crowd in the sticky smear of your soiled clothes. Your dejections cooled by the wind. To accept the marks, not only symbolic, of physical destitution. That is the body as it is—given, in the making, crumbly.

13
Trace

Now that, after fighting hard and long, I can no longer ignore the effects of time on my cycling powers, now that the ugly face of age has caught me in its jaws and forced me to stare at the damage, it hurts here and it hurts there and I only train inconsistently. It leaves a hint of sadness on my tongue and I'm always tempted by denial. From time to time, I still have passionate plans to give up everything and ride again as if anything were still possible and to get away from my fears of having to count my steps. A hundred kilometers a day, no less. Green beans, no more wine. Of course, the flow of daily emotions brings me brutally back to reason like the ocean, with a casual wave, takes back the shipwrecked sailor who thought he had found his footing on the sand and was aiming at distant lights. The sea is rolling me around and wearing me out. Still, when it manages to lick its wounds on the beach, my reminiscent body still surprises me at times. I remain inclined to my small devotions and I still happen to jump on my bike after watching a race on television, for fear of letting a moment of efficient inspiration slip away, the same way as we sometimes look for a piece of paper in our pockets to write down an idea we are bound to forget. And it works quite well. It does not last long, but for a few kilometers, for an hour or so, I impersonate with some credibility the haughty figures of the champions. I could almost bury my face in my hands, as if injured, as if I feared losing the images stuck to my eyes and that give my legs the right attitude. I fear the end of the spell. And it always comes. I also know that as the years go by, I will need more images to inspire me on the same distance. I know that I will have to be dedicated in my little spiritual exercises to remember in my legs what it means to be a rider. My timid attempts to embody the cycling show may be ridiculous. And I am not certain that they do not rest on an illusion. But on that road and in those ruts that I am starting to be afraid of, they are an infinitely better consolation than the pseudo knowledge, crammed with stats and figures, that pretends to be describing performance these days.

Physical decline leads to the quest of other acmes, otherwise life would be unbearable. I am reaching the point where every one of us looks back and stares at the undecipherable appearance of the path behind and bravely tries to believe that we are starting to understand. Still it is difficult for me to have a clear view of what will remain of all those efforts and what trace they will leave in my body once it becomes incapable of reproducing them. Even in the event that my mind stays clear, the fact of not pedaling anymore will turn my existence into a residue.

My view on cycling is the same as Leonardo da Vinci's view on painting: it is a *cosa mentale*. Its physical dimension is secondary. While now sport is always expressed through mathematical data (how fanciful . . .) and while the performance of riders is evaluated with all sorts of quantitative gear, we do mistake the action for its trace, the hard work for the object it creates. Of course data are very important for coaches, but however useful as tools, the obsession with figures amounts to a strange process of embalming. It really looks as though the measurement of performance is seen as more real than the performance itself. Being the natural enemy of words (which vaguely and endlessly attempt to create meaning), measuring annihilates the possibility of a tale. But performance as it is created and updated is nothing else but the frame of mind of the athlete producing it: its reality lies in the curtain of trees seen in the distant gray sky, in a fleeting memory, in the holy feeling of muscular warmth. To pedal is to give a meaning to things, nothing more and nothing less. Cycling is a privileged way to inhabit that place where images are created. It is irrelevant that this operation of the mind should spend energy in the physical space. And cycling is no more a sport than the paintings of Caravaggio are pretty: that is rubbish.

Not that cycling has nothing to do with beauty. Quite the opposite: beauty is the very principle of cycling. I always thought that an ugly rider could not go fast. That efficient riders, while not always the most nicely built, always radiate, one way or another, with great elegance. And also that seeing them pedal inspires an emotion quite similar or in line with the sentiment of beauty. However there are always some exceptions to the rule, which, as the saying goes, are meant to confirm it.

The exception is not a minor one, since Chris Froome, the best Tour de France rider of recent years, an athlete with indisputable qualities, displays a style that is detrimental to the iconic value of the champion. The moments when he is the most impressive are precisely when he is the ugliest. On climbs, his obvious superiority seems to contradict even the laws of vision. Above his hands placed on the handlebars, he pedals with his arms extremely spread apart, with one shoulder bent lower and one elbow sticking out more than the other. You almost expect to see him move sideways and out of the focus of the camera. With his skinny arms and his sharp elbows turned upside down, he looks like a kind of spider. When, after looking down at his feet for a moment, he raises his head, his face moves to the side and if he stands up on his pedals to attack, the extraordinary cadences he is known for make it impossible for him to straighten up completely. He looks as if he is pedaling in the void. His chest does not stretch, his head never seems to move apart from the shoulders and that hunched-up attitude looks quite uncomfortable. Froome is a stylistic heresy who contradicts my profession of faith of *kalos kagathos* or "beauty is efficient," according to which style is the only thing that matters.

While he is not anymore his most dangerous opponent because his career is behind him, Alberto Contador was the exact opposite of Froome. Not only because he is Latin and Catholic, when Froome's domination is issued from the Anglo-Saxon and Protestant culture, which currently dominates cycling. Strictly in terms of movements, their styles clashed totally. While Froome seems to suffer a lot even when he drops all his rivals, Contador, on the other hand, almost loses nothing of his impressive elegance when he falters. We can only notice, in the painful moments that seem to never end for a cyclist, when he tries to hold a pace he cannot match, that the movement of his bike becomes a bit shaky. Just a bit. When at the top of his game he goes into incredibly long accelerations *en danseuse*. And then the swinging motion of his bike is a wonder of fluidity. From the axis around which his feet gravitate like satellites in an amazingly even rotation, so consistent it is hard to distinguish periods, his two wheels rock from left to right and follow on the road a perfectly natural course. Swift and fast, his bike glides ahead like a snake. When Alberto cracks, or fades, a few binary elements seem about to appear in that almost perfect continuity. But that is all. The rocking of the bike becomes slightly exaggerated and takes a little more space on the road. But that jerky impression remains discreet, only a hint. It never really happens.

Mountain climbs are their terrain of excellence. But the effort they require is very specific and involves as much delicacy as determination. If we accept, without claiming to replace the intensity training scales used by coaches, to split effort into levels, we could consider that the first one is the equivalent of a gentle ride and that the last, the seventh heaven (and the most common intensity scale used by coaches, the ESIE scale, has seven degrees) coincides with the pure burst of energy, the sheer excitement of sprinting. While the efforts that can be sustained for a long time, several hours, place the rider in a disposition of patient, almost monotonous repetition, the efforts that can be upheld only for a few seconds are akin to a scream.

Of course this upscale course takes into account the relativity of the perception of time; to ride for five hours does sometimes not appear "longer" than the most crucial minute of the race, the moment when everything is at stake, when everything is decided. To say that a minute or fifteen seconds seem "never-ending" is not only a stylistic device. Between the two poles of intensity takes place a real upheaval of eternity, which shifts from the horizontality of the outside terrain to the inner verticality of the crucial moment. A shift from visual depth to spiritual depth, in the emergency of effort.

It is not astonishing, along the way, to come across areas of turbulence (which the specialists divide into three categories they call "critical," "subcritical," and "submaximal") that require a strange disposition of the mind based on the subtle control of moods. It consists in maintaining with the utmost care and during a few minutes the effects of the initial scream, of the initial release of violence imposed on one's body. To feed—think of the wall of clenched jaws opening the way for the pack at the bottom of a climb—that aggression as consistently as possible to delay the arrival of pain and to resist it. You must get angry. Very angry but not too much. Because the trick of the trade is that you must proceed on a tightrope, which is both tricky and fearsome. Aggression is necessary but getting carried away is fatal. You must take the pain close to unbearable and still avoid tackling it frontally, and you can only do that spurred by a form of anger, but you cannot afford to lose it completely. The slightest miscalculation, the slightest outburst condemns the climber to falter and give up. That is when you see the most furious, the most hyperactive riders suddenly stall and sit back heavily in the saddle, suddenly stuck, hapless.

From one second to the next, the pedaling dancer finds himself glued to the slope like on flypaper.

Riding between harrowing pain and the threatening ghost of failure, between the burning flame and the attraction of the void, the one assigned to that mission plays a very delicate role. To climb a mountain at full gas relies on the body, of course. But it is fundamentally a spiritual exercise. Spiritual acrobatics. The top climber does not only ride on the edge of a blade, he nurtures conflicting inclinations, forced as he is to conciliate modesty and fury. Torn between ancient hubris and Christian humility, he can be described as a humble genius. Hence the tragic masks, the wrathful or sorry grins, spontaneous and haphazard character studies of rage and suffering, of Homeric flashes and resigned agony.

And since there is no soul without a body, it is understandable that such a revealing effort should be a perfect showcase of style. As unsightly as Froome might be, and he is, I am not aesthetically indifferent to the spectacle of his amazing accelerations. His heron legs reel at an unusual, almost ridiculous speed and I cannot help but deplore the nod. And yet, after a few seconds, when his attack is launched and he is going full gas, it moves me. It is not such a violent, frank, and rough emotion but it is very real. It is not gut-wrenching or heart-rending as is for me the vision of the Praxiteles of the sport, I mean

Anquetil, Merckx, De Vlaeminck, or Contador, in a way. It is not love at first sight. But it overwhelms me patiently and emerges after a few turns taken at full speed by the odd style of the Briton. The beauty I am talking about is not mimetic, it does not relate to vision but to a form of empathy. Froome is beautiful in my eyes because he rides fast and because I can feel—my eyes half-closed because they would be useless in this case—the huge pleasure he must feel. And I feel the same because I can picture his sensations. I can feel the handlebars in my palms, my feet picking up the carbon soles of my shoes and the vibration of the road. I can feel the elevation of the Ventoux and the formidable push also seizes me by the guts and the groin. I could almost find myself breathless without moving.

Strictly speaking I indulge in exercises of devotion quite similar to those recommended by Ignatius of Loyola and which gave birth to an entire tradition of paintings meant to support them. Pictures, images designed to boost effort. The slight difference being that I am not trying to suffer like Christ but to share the same delights as the champions.

This ambivalent way of looking at things combines the results of physical vision and those of imagination. At the junction of those two ways of seeing emerge various theories on the efficiency of beauty that are not that grotesque. While the eugenic obsession that pushed Nazis to surround Aryan women with Greek statues to make sure they produced "beautiful" children was close to demented, we cannot deny that the active contemplation of things can influence our capacities.

It is something I have verified more than once: watching a segment of a race with your eyes half-closed, so that the image comes through but not its outlines, in order to retain only the essence of movement, the movement itself, not personified, improves the quality of your own movements. And I owe some of my progression (let alone my passion) to the outstanding motricity of champions. I trained hard in my teens after watching Hinault in Sallanches, Fignon sprint up l'Alpe d'Huez, allowing himself brief moments of freewheeling in the corners! The unlikely exploits of the riders on EPO inspired me all the same. Mayo on the Ventoux was sublime. Ullrich at Arcalis, Pantani, Bartoli, Vandenbroucke on La Redoute, again and forever. It is a long list. Also comes, not to my mind but to my whole body, the amazing skillfulness of Peter Van Petegem; he was filmed from the back and his back wheel was floating and slaloming on the *pavé* in the cobbled sector of L'Arbre, and I know that each time I ride there again myself it will bring back that memory and help me find the right posture. Those images are driving forces. It is a well-known fact but astonishing all the same. I imagine that neurologists have an explanation based on "neuronal mirrors" and that psychologists and coaches evoke suggestion and visualization. But what we are talking about is the power of images and the direct power of their meaning on the body.

Of course it is probably easier to welcome the demon of racing when, like me, you have some experience of it. Because there is a path, a trail to follow. I still dream about my past races and, to be honest, I mostly go through my anxieties again. From the bottom of my skull, my eyes closed, I can feel the rain whip my cheekbones and my legs roll beneath the soaking shorts, I feel my hands go numb on the handlebars and, stretching my neck and slightly moving it aside, I adapt my effort to the sidewinds, fighting my way into the echelon against the sweet shoulder of my girlfriend. I wake in sweat and desolation, nauseous at the smell of warm-up creams and iodine solutions, while countless ankles of luminescent foam vanish across the ceiling in this up-and-down movement that paced my entire life. I am alone. The peloton has gone and I must live by myself, cut away from it, *in vitro*. I take the sheet aside and I move my hands across my lost body, my skinny legs, my fat belly, my hairy chest, even the skin beneath my testicles is not the same any more, that patch of satin worn out by mileage of which I was always ready to talk, to say something funny about my rider's condition. I could almost start to cry, but once the surprise of waking up is gone, I can feel it fitting again in the darkness of the room, in the cellar of my lungs and around my bones. My body settles back in and I sink confidently into absence. The rider in me is a trace. So deep that should my body melt completely, it would still be there.

14

The Old Man

In the club of my childhood, the first rides of the winter always involved riders of all categories and all ages. It was team spirit, comradeship, maybe even brotherhood. While our levels were quite different, we always made sure for a few sessions to stay together and to form coherent bunches as safe as warm stomachs moving around the freezing countryside. You always ride along with the elders with a cautious curiosity, afraid your time will come too and also comforted by their presence because age gaps are unbeatable.

I remember a man I'm going to name because I saw him at the time as in a kind of mirror. I was starting in the trade, so to speak, while his career, admittedly, was behind him. Still he went on riding thanks to a doctor who kept signing his license in spite of notorious heart problems. But the old Bretelle was a cyclist, that was all he was, and it would have killed him to stop riding.

The Old Man

That morning, it struck him inadvertently as he was polishing his bike like he had done for the past forty-five years—because going for a training ride on a dirty bike is unacceptable. He had looked through the window. Small gardening lots were growing on the hill above the railway and light seemed to be pouring from the blossoming pear trees.

Sun, tender and lively hearth
Pours its burning love on the delighted earth . . .

The man was a hard-boiled rider who had lived only for the sake of pinning a bib on his back. He smelled of camphor and firewood. But, and it came as a surprise to me, the only thing he remembered from the remote times when he used to go to school was poetry. All the rest he had forgotten (if you failed to notice that he could read and count and that you could not fool him around easily) and everything he knew he had learned from the bike and women. That was the way he put it. All the rest, except poetry. Not that he could recite a long poem. But sometimes, on a ride, he would remember a couple of verses, a stanza perhaps, learned when his parents were still around, when he was a kid, when his eyes were mobile and bright. And as I was watching his ankles, as knotty as the trunk of an old olive tree, I was telling myself that maybe one day I would look the same. Mad and definite.

The Old Man

His keys would rattle in his pocket every time he cautiously ignored red lights and started again on his beautiful bike. Throughout his life, he had only white bicycles. "I'm faithful to my first love," he said, rolling his glass eye, and he always took the same pleasure at looking down to see it rock gently between his expert legs. His knees were moving up and down as if operating the heavy chain—unfurling and squeaking on its pulley in the middle of the night—at the bottom of which was hanging a bucketful of vivid memories. Poetry was definitely language and he made believe he was not too good at that game. But the idea he had of poets and that he was sharing with them was a sense of wonderment at the coming of spring. The viridian surge, the burgeoning, the powerful scent of the earth at sunset gripping the throat. For him, human's need for poetry lay there, in that painful emotion—spring is marvelous, breathtaking. And it is the season of the first races.

That Sunday, everything was singing around him on the road, the light was falling between tender leaves and sizzling like petals on the undergrowth soil so that it seemed as though his front wheel was turning backward, the wind was blue and strong still, the smells fresh. Nothing was yet announcing the lingering marble skies of summer.

He was riding with his pals, with his clubmates. Working-class sportsmen, forever young. His blushing cheekbones were two cherries beneath the wrinkled eyelids sheltering both his eyes, the living and the dead. He was smiling, blissful, showing a mask of teeth as he peered through the trees at a God he did not believe in. Spring and its empty sky spread over the countryside, and what he would have liked to do was not to write rhymes about them, not to hug them, but to swallow them. To fill himself up to the brim. The whole sky and the clouds without choking, with the trees and the cheeping birds, the fresh earth and the moss—only happiness could have stopped him from gulping. I imagine he was wearing the same old beret I always saw him ride with, slightly sideways, the tip at the top discreetly out of line. Never a helmet ever in his life, except in races when the rules imposed it. When he was not pedaling, he would ride along with us on a vintage scooter. A hand in his pocket, the other on the handle, he would stay at your level, scrutinizing you so closely that even his rudimentary glass eye seemed alive. Then, after a few grins of approbation, he would tell you tales of races and prostitutes as if he had ridden them all, known them all.

As always, he was madly happy to ride. Even if the pace imposed by the kids, by his young colleagues, did not make it easy for the old man to laugh out loud. He was beginning to wane a bit as a rider. Still there was no changing the rules of his existence. So he would not agree to go on holiday before winning a race. At least one, even a small one. He would train a little bit harder in the weeks to come. At least three eighty-mile sessions, yeah, and he would also take the old fixie out. That's what he was saying for the umpteenth time, pedaling with his chest high, a hand on the next guy's shoulder as he was chatting with him while controlling the wheel with slight movements of the hip.

That's when it struck. It first rocked the bike. He grabbed the handlebars, but it did not let go. He swerved around softly, a few times, like a clown taking the time to announce his fall by riding along the wooden ridge of the track on which he is about to collapse. He lost balance and it laid him down sweetly and it lay upon his body, its open mouth on his. Suddenly dumb, he found himself lying there. His bare legs on the road and his neck on the cool blue watercress. He was still smiling, his long figure stretched amid the scattered bikes thrown around him by his frightened comrades. He had kept his promise or it had. It had come to take him at the agreed meeting place, on his eternal white bike, and the time did not matter. A circle of dazed faces, the translucent green of the treetops, the blue sky and its pitch-black flipside. In the ditch, the wheel of the bike was still turning and playing to his ears the swift music of the freewheel, clear on the hoarse background sound of singing birds, wardens of the world.

The Old Man

They say that his pals also kept their word as they dressed him up for his last appointment. He was put in the box in the club's outfit, with two bars of fruit jelly for the race. He did not look deader than usual; he looked brand new. Only the polystyrene chips were missing to wrap up the parcel.

Of course we all tried, each in our own mind, to visualize him sliding across the black water to the other side, his back hunching a bit, sitting at the prow of the boat, his knee trembling, holding his bike by his side. His beret on his head, his mittens on his hands, on his feet his white socks and the freshly waxed pair of his most beautiful Dello Pietros. And finally four safety pins and a bib on his back. I could not see the number.

A Univocal Book

Drew S. Burk, Consulting Editor

Univocal Publishing was founded by Jason Wagner and Drew Burk as an independent publishing house specializing in artisanal editions and translations of texts spanning the areas of cultural theory, media archeology, continental philosophy, aesthetics, anthropology, and more. In 2017, Univocal ceased operations as an independent publishing house and became a series with its publishing partner, the University of Minnesota Press.

Univocal Authors

Miguel Abensour
Judith Balso
Jean Baudrillard
Philippe Beck
Simon Critchley
Fernand Deligny
Jacques Derrida
Vinciane Despret
Georges Didi-Huberman
Jean Epstein
Vilém Flusser
Barbara Glowczewski
Évelyne Grossman
Félix Guattari
Olivier Haralambon
David Lapoujade
François Laruelle
David Link
Sylvère Lotringer

Jean Malaurie
Michael Marder
Serge Margel
Quentin Meillassoux
Friedrich Nietzsche
Peter Pál Pelbart
Jacques Rancière
Lionel Ruffel
Felwine Sarr
Michel Serres
Gilbert Simondon
Étienne Souriau
Isabelle Stengers
Sylvain Tesson
Eugene Thacker
Antoine Volodine
Elisabeth von Samsonow
Siegfried Zielinski

Fascinated by bicycle racing since he was thirteen years old, OLIVIER HARALAMBON was a racing cyclist for ten years, riding in hundreds of races. He studied philosophy at the University of Paris XII and also was a sports journalist. He is the author of four books.

RICHARD MOORE is a freelance sports journalist, former racing cyclist, and cohost, with Lionel Birnie and Daniel Friebe, of The Cycling Podcast. He has written seven books on bicycle racing.

FRANÇOIS THOMAZEAU is a French sports journalist, translator, publisher, musician, and renowned crime novelist.